SHADES AND STYLES OF

P9-EJH-683

DATE DUE

NO 1 '99			
AP 0 '00			
AP 24 '00			

The Shapes and Styles of
Asian American Prose Fiction

American University Studies

Series XXIV
American Literature

Vol. 42

PETER LANG
New York • San Francisco • Bern • Baltimore
Frankfurt am Main • Berlin • Wien • Paris

Esther Mikyung Ghymn

The Shapes and Styles of Asian American Prose Fiction

PETER LANG
New York • San Francisco • Bern • Baltimore
Frankfurt am Main • Berlin • Wien • Paris

Library of Congress Cataloging-in-Publication Data

Ghymn, Esther Mikyung.
   The shapes and styles of Asian American prose fiction / Esther
Mikyung Ghymn.
      p. cm. — (American university studies. Series XXIV, American
literature; vol. 42)
   Includes bibliographical references.
      1. American fiction—Asian American authors—History and
criticism.   2. Asian Americans—Intellectual life.   3. Asian
Americans in literature.   I. Title.   II. Series.
PS153.A84G48   1992   810.9′.895—dc20   92-8720
ISBN 0-8204-1919-2   CIP
ISSN 0895-0512

Die Deutsche Bibliothek-CIP-Einheitsaufnahme

Ghymn, Esther Mikyung:
The shapes and styles of Asian American prose fiction / Esther
Mikyung Ghymn.—New York; Berlin; Bern; Frankfurt/M.; Paris;
Wien: Lang, 1992
   (American university studies : Ser. 24, American literature ; Vol. 42)
   ISBN 0-8204-1919-2
NE: American university studies/24

The paper in this book meets the guidelines for permanence and
durability of the Committee on Production Guidelines for
Book Longevity of the Council on Library Resources.

© Peter Lang Publishing, Inc., New York 1992

Printed in the United States of America.

Table of Contents

Acknowledgments

I owe my greatest debt to my father, Kim Yong Shik, who has always encouraged me in my literary pursuits.

My special thanks to Robert Merrill, director of my dissertation, for his invaluable guidance and careful reading of the manuscript. I would also like to thank Randall Reid, Susan Baker, and Daulatram Lund for their helpful suggestions and insights. I would also like to express my appreciation to Ann Ronald for providing me with valuable bibliographical information.

I am also grateful to my husband, Kyung-Il, and my children, Jennifer and Eugene, for their support.

Dedication

To My Father and the Memory of My Mother

Chapter One

Introduction

The study of Asian American literature is a new development in the field of American literature. Despite the fact that Asian Americans have lived in this country for more than one hundred and forty years, there are only one or two books on Asian American literature on most university shelves. Until recently this body of writing has been ignored by most critics who believe that it lacks aesthetic value. Linguistic and cultural barriers have also hindered the recognition of Asian American literature. Today, however, it seems evident that Asian American literature is beginning to find its rightful place.

Thus far, the few existing studies have emphasized the sociological and historical background of the relevant works while offering general summaries of individual texts. The purpose of this study is to examine the artistic qualities of the works selected. This study is undertaken with Percy Lubbock's words in mind: "The author of the book was a craftsman, the critic must overtake him at his work and see how the book was made." (Lubbock, p. 274) To do this, however, we must understand the cultural context in which such books were made. According to Henry James, "a novel is in its broadest definition a personal, direct impression of life." If we accept this definition, we should try to understand the personal and cultural background of these "impressions." Some background needs to be provided so that a reader unfamiliar with Asian customs will be able to understand the significance and symbolism of certain situations in the novels. As Hsaio-min Han points out, "A large number of Asian American literary works are deeply concerned with immigration experiences, with special emphasis on the inevitable conflict between Asiatic mother culture and the new American culture. Without a considerable understanding of these Oriental cultures, the reader very often misses some of the profound and most enjoyable parts of the literature." (Han, p. 6) I do not believe that the reader needs a "considerable" understanding; however, a brief explanation will be included when necessary.

At this point I think it is appropriate to include an overview of the critical works that have focused mainly on the sociological and cultural features of Asian American literature. In her preface to *Asian American Literature*, Elaine Kim states, "For the purposes of this study, however, I have deliberately chosen to emphasize how the literature elucidates the social history of Asians in the United States. The problem of understanding Asian American literature within its sociohistorical and cultural contexts is important to me because, when these contexts are unfamiliar, the literature is likely to be misunderstood and unappreciated. But the fact that this book is not an attempt to appreciate the formal literary merit of Asian American literature does not mean that I see no value in formal and stylistic interpretations; it only means that such interpretations were not my intention here. I feel certain that there are many more competent than I who will continue to address this question." (Kim, *Asian American Literature*, p. xv) Kim's work provides a very useful introduction to Asian American literature. Her social perspective gives us a strong historical and social context; however, Kim is a social historian at the University of California, Berkeley, and her study does not include detailed literary analysis.

Stephen Sumida, in his review of Kim's work, remarks, "Elaine H. Kim's book has been called the first full-length literary study of Asian American fiction, poetry, drama, and autobiography. But it is neither the first nor strictly speaking a literary study." (Sumida, p. 106) Sumida further points out, "Kim's method is to preface or to weave into her interpretations sociological and historical commentary indicating 'how the literature elucidates the social history of Asians in the United States'.... It may be more accurate to say that Kim uses literature mainly to illustrate sociohistorical assumptions about

Asian Americans." (Sumida, pp. l06-l07) Sumida's points are perceptive. The web of symbols and images which frames the design of a novel should not be designated as secondary in the study of literature.

Further studies of Asian American literature have also avoided concentrating on the artistic elements of literary works. In 1974 a group of militant writers published a book called Aiiieeeee. Frank Chin and others in its preface presented what Kim calls "a manifesto for a new direction in Asian American culture. Taking as a symbol of their effort Kwan Kung, Chinese god of art and war ... they asserted, [that it] expressed the genuine spirit of Asian American history and culture and not the old stereotypes that had held sway for so long." (Kim, *Asian American Literature*, p. l73) Chin's work is punctuated with angry references to racial discrimination. Han believes the study is seriously flawed. "Led by Frank Chin, the militant group of Chinatown authors is relatively younger, rebellious, and further away from Chinese culture than the former group .... Many of them were educated in the United States and have not had much formal learning in Chinese language and culture .... On the one hand, their limited Chinese education and, probably, the generation gap, made the traditional idea of cultural supremacy seem remote and unrealistic to them. On the other hand, their American education did not succeed in making them believe that Chinese Americans are culturally in the melting pot." (Han, p. 33) Han's observations are all too true. *Aiiieeeee* is an anthology of works by Asian Americans who were born or raised in this country, and its contents suggest many other limitations. The *Big Aiiieeeee* by the same editors, Jeffrey Paul Chan, Frank Chin, Lawson Fusao Inada, and Shawn Wong, was published in 1991. Indeed, aside from the comments in the prefaces, these books can hardly be called literary studies.

William Wu in *The Yellow Peril: Chinese American in American Fiction 1850-1940* (1982) states that the image of the Chinese in American fiction has been that of "the yellow peril." Wu concentrates on the racial image of his people, not the literary value of the books. Other critics such as Haslam, Baker, Fisher, Lim, Wang, and Hsu have discussed Asian American writing in their books; however, none has focused primarily on its aesthetic qualities. By contrast, two doctoral dissertations in the 1980s advanced the study of Asian American literature. In her dissertation *Roots and Buds* (1980), Hsaio-min Han at Brigham Young University classifies Asian American writers into four groups: "early immigrant writers," "sojourner writers," "Chinatown writers," and "intelligentsia writers." Han discusses the historical background and broad literary characteristics of each group. This method of formal definition is useful because it provides a good introduction to Asian American literature. As her title indicates, her argument seems to be that contemporary Asian American literature owes a lot to its roots. Han's work is useful because it gives the reader a basic background to the field.

Ruth Hsaio in her dissertation *The Stages of Development in American Ethnic Literature: Jewish and Chinese American Literatures* (1982) labels her "stages" under the following titles: "Insider/Outsider: The Immigrant Writer," "The American Self: Participant in the Mainstream," "The Integrated Self: Artist Quester." Hsiao's categories are thought-provoking, but I don't think that they are very precise. For example, the integrated self is not a condition for the artist quester, nor is the cause and effect relationship expressed in her titles logical. She states, "The stages of development advanced by this study are defined according to the evolving self presented in writings because ethnic literature is always largely about the process of finding self." (Hsaio, p. 12) I disagree with her premise. The primary purpose of literature is not self-realization nor is it a kind of self-therapy. I also disagree with Hsiao's next statement about the first stage of development: "The deracinated self of this stage tries to mediate between two cultures and two worlds, but feels that it is an outsider to both." (Hsaio, p. 28) I believe that the early writers were firmly planted in their native cultures. This firm foundation gave the early writers the confidence and strength to write in English despite seemingly insurmountable obstacles. Hsaio asserts that in the second stage "the ethnic writer is sufficiently independent that he/she quarrels with both worlds, protesting their oppressiveness." (Hsaio, p. 28) In the third stage, "the self fully realizes its creativity in fashioning its own selfhood and its own art for the expressed purpose of truth finding." (Hsaio, p. 29) In the final stage, "the self freely searches for fruitful connections with its dual world and consolidates its dual allegiance as a means of achieving integration in the fragmented modern world." (Hsaio, p. 29) The problem with her thesis is the implied assumption that only favorable social conditions produce good artists, an example of "post hoc, ergo propter hoc" logic.

The studies mentioned above focus on the sociological background of the works. To me that is like looking at Picasso's "La Toilette" or "Les Desmoiselles d'Aignon" and stating that the period in which he lived is the work's primary cause. Such an assumption takes away from the artist's significance. Likewise it is like listening to the "Requiem Mass" by Mozart and saying that the conditions of the years 1756-1791 are responsible for his music. Finally, it is like touching the smooth carving of "Pieta" or the handsome face of "Brutus" by Michelangelo and saying that these works were created because the artist lived during the Renaissance. One should not deny the artist his talent. The works of Picasso, Mozart, and Michelangelo are the products of their own genius and training. The writers addressed in this study may not equal these exalted artists, but their better works deserve to be read as literary achievements first and cultural artifacts second.

At this point it is perhaps relevant to introduce a brief historical background on Asian American literature before defining its major literary features. The early Asian American writers were an elite group. The majority of Asians in the early nineteenth century were recruited from villages and towns in Asia to build railroads and mines on the West Coast. The Asian population was predominantly male although some women entered the United States as picture brides. Asians faced severe discrimination not only from the general population but as a result of legislation. Laws such as the Chinese Exclusion Act of 1882 prohibited the immigration of laborers. In 1913 the Alien Land Law Act prevented Asians from owning any land. Furthermore the Asian Exclusion Act of 1924 prohibited intermarriage between Asians and Americans, and

denied citizenship rights to immigrant Chinese and Japanese.
In 1942, after the Japanese bombed Pearl Harbor, Japanese
Americans were sent to relocation camps. In 1943 the Chinese
Exclusion Act was repealed, but only in 1952 were Japanese
Americans granted citizenship. Thus the early Asian American
writers wrote during a period of severe discrimination. Early
writers like Lin Yu Tang, Younghill Kang, and Chin Yang
Lee drew upon their inner resources to counter the fact that
Asians in most American fiction were presented as stereotypes
and comical caricatures. Kim points out that "Stock Chinese
brutes and villains abound in a large body of short stories and
novels set in Chinatowns of the West from the latter part of
the 19th century until the 1940s." (Kim, *Asian American Literature*, p. 10) At this time the American public knew very little
about Asian Americans. As Kim goes on to note, "Even Bret
Harte, Mark Twain, and Ambrose Bierce, who are said to have
portrayed the Chinese sympathetically, accepted most of the
common stereotypes of the Chinese of their times and knew
little or nothing of the reality of Chinese life in America."
(Kim, *Asian American Literature*, p. 14)

In many of the early portrayals the source of the humor was
the characters' use of the English language. "To generations
of Americans, on the other hand, Chinese English meant 'no
tickee, no washee.' A mainstay of popular American culture,
the comic Chinese dialect is characterized by high-pitched,
sing-song tones, tortured syntax, the confounding of l's and r's,
the proliferation of ee-endings, and the random omission of
articles and auxiliary verbs." (Kim, *Asian American Literature*, p.
12) By contrast, early Asian American writers like Kim Yong
Ik wanted their characters to speak like true Koreans; Kim
himself wanted the public to see the real world of Koreans.
Chin Yang Lee portrayed a Chinese family speaking Chinese
English. His motive, however, was not to provoke laughter at
the characters, but to preserve their idiomatic expressions.

Critics have disagreed about the definition of Asian American literature. As Kim states, "the term Asian American is a
controversial one ... we are accepting an externally imposed
label that is meant to define us by distinguishing us from other
Americans primarily on the basis of race rather than culture."

(Kim, *Asian American Literature*, p. xii) Chin wants the term Asian American to include only those who are born or raised in this country: "The age, variety, depth, and quality of the writing collected here proves the existence of Asian-American sensibilities and cultures that might be related to but are distinct from Asia and white America." (Chin, p. viii) For the purpose of this study, Asian American literature will be defined as significant writings by American writers of Asian heritage. When an Asian becomes a naturalized United States citizen, he is classified as an Asian American. Therefore, if we are to adopt the premise of this legal definition, Asian American literature should not be limited to the works by writers born in this country.

In order to sample the different artistic shapes and fictional worlds of Asian American literature as defined above, I have selected for study two Chinese American writers, one Japanese American writer, and two Korean American writers. This study therefore resembles books on American literature that examine some of its major writers. The writings of Hawthorne, Poe, Melville, Hemingway, and Updike are different; together, however, they represent the different faces of American literature. Poe is not expected to represent the general characteristics of most writers in his period. Likewise, Nabokov does not represent all white Russian writers, and Joseph Conrad cannot be viewed as a typical Polish English writer. Neither American nor Asian American literature can be fitted into a neat box, nor can its development be sketched in a straight line. Likewise the works of the five writers in this study exhibit quite different styles and structures.

This study of five Asian Americans will reveal their individual talents as well as the real worlds they represent. As Jessamym West suggests, "Fiction reveals truths that reality obscures." By depicting and drawing from their own experiences these writers dramatize important truths about the Asian American existence. The five writers are Chin Yang Lee, an early Chinese American writer; Kim Yong Ik, an early Korean American writer; Richard Kim, a Korean existential writer; Yoshiko Uchida, a Japanese American author of juvenile stories, and Maxine Hong Kingston, a contemporary Chinese American writer.

The characters of Chinatown in Chin Yang Lee's novels, the tortured lovers in a Korean village in Kim Yong Ik's stories, the desperate victims of the Korean War, the strong and weak women of Kingston's world, and the lonely Japanese family in a concentration camp all form individual stories. However, together they are like different sounds from the same orchestra. The purpose of this study is to analyze how the different sounds are made. The main focus will not be on the experience of the cultural background itself but on how the writer has reproduced it in novel form. The individual impressions derived from these experiences constitute, as James states, "an immense sensibility in a huge spiderweb of the silken threads suspended in the chamber of consciousness." The delicate threads of Asian American prose fiction will be separated and examined under a literary microscope.

In order to appreciate the "silken threads suspended in the chamber of consciousness" the critic should have some knowledge of Asian and Asian American thought and language. Without such a background, one cannot entirely disentangle the forms, structures, and themes of the works. In 1987 when I was teaching comparative literature at Yonsei University in Seoul to a group of American exchange students, one of the students thought that the theme of "The Wedding Shoes" was a man's abnormal obsession with shoes. Deconstructive critics might support the student's right to interpret the story according to his own understanding. However, the student's interpretation was certainly not what the writer intended. Kim Yong Ik intended to write an authentic, tragic Korean love story. In order to do that he used the shoes as a thematic and structural device. I believe that being a Korean American myself helps me achieve a fuller understanding of the stories.

There are also several instances in the stories where a knowledge of the Korean language helps. In Kim Yong Ik's "From Here You Can See the Moon" the narrator recalls, "No face I knew; nor did any face know me." A reader might think that Kim was employing a conventional synecdoche. However, the passage is a word for word translation from

Korean. In Korean the word "face" sometimes stands for a person. Even the title "From Here You Can See the Moon" is a translation of the title of a poem that the author wrote as a child. Kim's frequent use of Korean expressions heightens the authenticity of his stories. In his study of Asian American authors, Hsu points out, "They want white Americans to see beauty in the brown and yellow and respond to their language, Asian American language, to its metaphors they may seem quaint or ungrammatical by a white American standard but that sensitively reflect their unique experience and mirror their world." (Hsu, p. 5)

Furthermore, an understanding of Asian or Asian American values is helpful. Different values are the root causes of different concepts of pride, for example. Pride in turn is the key ingredient in most formal tragedies. Thus, without a knowledge of the value system in a story it is difficult for a reader to decipher a writer's intentions. For me Kim's stories are real tragedies. In addition, the village described in the stories is not some imaginary faraway place. I have been to that village many times as my ancestors have lived there for four hundred years. The father that the author describes in "From Here You Can See the Moon" is my grandfather: Kim Yong Ik is my uncle. Although I left Korea when I was an infant, I think my Korean background helps me to penetrate the sensibilities of a Korean American writer. I have also lived in Tokyo and Hong Kong for more than five years. Thus, Uchida's happy world reminds me of my childhood in Tokyo. Furthermore, the scenes in *The Woman Warrior* are very real to me. The first words of the book are "You must not tell anyone,' my mother said." This admonition is very Asian and familiar to me. Asian children are always told by their mothers to keep family secrets and wear a mask. I must believe that a study of an ethnic literature is best done by someone with a background in that culture.

The different stories by the different artists reveal the truth and spirit of Asian American experience. It is a challenging task to try to understand how these artists have created the shapes and structures of their more successful works. In the studies that follow I hope to do justice to the artistry that went into their making. The method used in this study will be to examine the following features: 1) the biographical background; 2) sociological and cultural factors that will help the reader understand the stories; 3) the structure of the writer's most significant work or works; 4) the work's principal characters; 5) individual style (images, sentence structures, rhetorical devices). Each of the five chapters will focus on one of the five major writers and will offer a structural analysis of the writer's most significant work or works, but character and stylistic analysis will be included as well. The organization will be chronological in order to suggest the basic development of Asian American prose fiction in subject matter and form. Brief comparison to American or European works will be included when applicable to provide additional insight into Asian American prose fiction.

Chapter Two

Chin Yang Lee:
Early Chinese American Writer

Chin Yang Lee, a well-known Chinese American writer, was born in Hunan, China in 1917. He came to the United States in 1943 and received his M.A. at Yale University. Best known for his first novel, *Flower Drum Song* (1957), which Rodgers and Hammerstein adopted into a musical play in 1959 and which Ross Hunter Productions then turned into a film, Lee is classified by Han as one of the "intelligentsia writers." (Han, p. 37) This is an appropriate classification because it places him with other educated writers who received graduate degrees in American universities. Lee is, indeed, a sophisticated artist. He carefully framed his best-known novel from structural principles based on the Horatian tradition (though he underplays Horace's insistence on "instruction"). It is fascinating to see how Lee combined ancient literary principles with contemporary Chinese American materials.

Lee's best work calls to mind one of the most delightful literary forms, the comedy of manners, and a Chinese American comedy of manners is an exquisite innovation. In the Horatian tradition the typical comedy of manners is amusing and pleasant. Lacking the harsh, even vicious thrust of Juvenalian satire, it offers witty and sparkling criticism of the social customs and manners of a certain group. Wit and mild irony make a comedy of manners sparkle and shine. These two techniques have proven invaluable for comedies from the Restoration period to modern times. The clever choice of words, the original juxtaposition of ideas or situations, the unexpected ending to a carefully delivered story invariably induce laughter. However, criticism remains the core of comedy. Without this core comedy has no purpose. Chin Yang Lee wrote *Flower Drum Song* with this aim in mind, carefully selecting the various scenes and language. As Werner Sollors says in his illuminating book *Beyond Ethnicity*, "The intensely ironic relationship of ethnic authors to in-group and out-group audiences, from both of whom they must have felt alienated at times, could also lend itself to a pioneering transcending leap ahead in literary form." (Sollors, p. 252) A Chinese American comedy of manners is such a creative venture and resulted in a highly acclaimed novel, a Broadway play, and a popular movie based primarily on the play.

Lee's comic structure provides the right framework for an objective portrait. Henry James would have approved. As James says, "We know a man imperfectly until we know his society, and we but half know a society, until we know its manners. This is especially true of a man of letters, for manners lie very close to literature." (Tuttleton, p. xi) Manners are indeed essential, and Lee paints them with bright and contrasting colors in his picture of vibrating Chinatown.

Some critics, however, fail to appreciate the Horatian quality in Lee's work. As Elaine Kim points out, "Contemporary Chinese American writers Frank Chin, Jeffrey Chan, and Shawn Hsu Wong have condemned *Flower Drum Song* as insulting and distortive of Chinese American life for the purpose of being acceptable or entertaining to the non-Chinese .... [For them] *Flower Drum Song* is an 'imported apothecary of ginseng and tuberculosis' that capitalizes on the 'chow mein-spaghetti' formula of the Chinatown books for 'bucks and popularity.'" (Kim, *Asian American Literature*, pp. 107-108) Perhaps this harsh criticism of Chin Yang Lee is due to the fact that for several decades the image of the Chinese in literature has been quite negative. Wu believes that "Yellow Peril is the overwhelming dominant theme in American fiction about Chinese Americans" (Wu, p. 2), fiction in which Chinese stereotypes are characterized most unattractively. The typical traits associated with the Chinese in literature have been stupidity and slyness, and the assigned roles are those of servants and murderers. Wu contends that the Chinese have always been regarded as threatening.

Lee is thought to be guilty of perpetuating just such strategies. Indeed, militant writers like Frank Chin do not understand Lee's artistic purpose. In their preface to their book *Aiiieeeee* (a word which means frustration in Chinese), they write, "Lee's *Flower Drum Song* affected our sensibility but did not express it." (Chin, p. x) Kim also agrees with this point of view: "Lee has the ability to do original research in Chinese and to write skillfully in English. However, he is apparently more interested in amusing and entertaining his readers by perpetuating their prejudices and ignorance than in the authentic presentation desired by the descendants of the figures at whose expense he writes." (Kim, *Asian American Literature*, p. 108) I disagree with this point of view. It is precisely Lee's English writing ability that brings his story and characters to life for a non-Chinese audience. His purpose in writing is not to perpetuate the reader's ignorance but to make the reader aware of the Chinese Americans in an entertaining manner.

I would also dispute another statement that Kim makes about *Flower Drum Song*: "Certainly humor is a dimension that should be vital in Asian American literature. The problem arises from the question of audience. In the vast body of existing stereotypes about Chinese, among which are euphemisms that discredit their experiences and dehumanize their lives, in light of the vast misunderstanding of Asian American life, one more book that perpetuates stereotypes has not been welcomed by Asian Americans seeking to break through the legacy of ignorance." (Kim, *Asian American Literature*, p. 107) Kim concedes that humor is an important ingredient in Asian American literature. However, it seems that she is really saying that Asian American literature has no place for humor because the audience has preconceived notions of the Chinese stereotypes. Therefore, if I follow her logic accurately, she is saying that comic portrayals perpetuate this negativism. She thinks that *Flower Drum Song* is "one more book that perpetuates stereotypes." Hsaio supports this contention. "[Lee's] Chinese characters, in general quaint and picturesque, speak mangled English, reinforcing the popular image of the Chinese the American public already held. This may account for the popularity of the book and subsequently the play. Both Lin [Yutang] and Lee exploited Chinatown for reasons other than responding to the problem of identity symbolized by the community." (Hsaio, p. 17)   But do all Chinese Americans have to write about the problem of identity? Lee's characters do speak broken English, but this is a realistic portrayal of their speech. Moreover, Hsaio's point applies far more to the play or film than to the novel. When the aunt in the movie version sings "Chop Suey" in broken English, when the father at first refuses to wear a western suit and when May Li discovers an American kiss for the first time, one can say the characterization is exaggerated. However, exaggeration is an essential element in many plays and movies. Visual movements and gestures are often repeated and exaggerated to make the audience understand. The novel, however, does not contain such hyperbolic actions.

At any rate, it is interesting to note that sometimes the Asian American audience is the hardest to please. Perhaps this negative reaction is due to the fact that Asian Americans have been too defensive about their self-image in literature, blinding them to a work's literary value. In some ways the non-Asian American audience is not as defensive and can appreciate the work from a more objective point of view. Critics like Chin and Kim seem all too self-conscious about social identity. Do all Chinese American writers have to promote social purposes? How dull literature would be if it were used to serve only political causes! Lee's intention was not simply to win the general public's approval and make money; rather, he wanted to entertain his audience and at the same time expose his non-Chinese audience to the customs and culture of the Chinese. Hsaio assumes that the underlying reason behind the book's success is its negative portrayal of the characters. This is an invalid indictment of the American audience. The stereotypes in previous works were created by the writers and not by the audience. Furthermore, Hsaio seems to be saying that the American audience as a whole is full of prejudice. If so, Americans are perhaps no different from anyone else. I remember Ian Watt's course on the comic novel at the University of Hawaii. During the first class Watt defined various types of comedy, then proceeded to explain Hobbes's characterization of human nature as evil. Because Hobbes is right, Watt explained, people laugh when they witness the misfortunes of fictional characters. Thus, we laugh at the Three Stooges and Laurel and Hardy. Whether or not Watt is right, I cannot agree with Hsaio that simplified characterization is the cause of the book's popularity. As Sloane says in *The Craft of Fiction*, "A character is never a whole person, but just those parts of him that fit the story of the piece of writing." (Sloane, p. 85) Critics should not judge characters as real persons divorced from the fictional world. I concur with Tuttleton "that a novel is a novel and not a piece of disguised sociology." (Tuttleton, p. xi) Characterization is only one of the parts of the engine that makes it run. Lee meticulously crafted all parts of his story to win the audience's approval.

The fact that Lee is able to look at his own people from a distance with wit and humor indicates how deep and confident his roots are in his own culture. Han points out that, "since most first generation Chinese Americans had their basic education in China, they naturally have a tendency to stick to that culture, and prejudiced attitudes cannot do much harm to them because, psychologically, they can always identify with this mother culture and find dignity and security there." (Han, p. 183) Lee finds it comfortable to write stories with strong plots because, in the Chinese tradition, there is more emphasis on the unraveling of problems and action than on the in-depth study of the characters. "Characterization in most Chinese novels usually lacks depth because the authors consider the narration of the actions more important than the development of fictive personalities .... The result is that the story is plot dominated and the characterization lacks profundity." (Han, p. 150) Lee studied literature intensively in China before he came to the United States, and it is not unreasonable to assume that Lee has been influenced by the Chinese literature he read. A closer look at *Flower Drum Song* supports this assumption, for plot is most important in this novel.

The setting of this novel is Chinatown. Hsaio mentions that "no study of an ethnic literature can be divorced from the milieu on which the writer bases and questions his identity.

For the case of Chinese American literature that place is Chinatown. This both looms symbolically as a reminder of the writer's ethnicity and also exists as actual place." (Hsaio, p. 16) Kim is resentful that Lee uses Chinatown as a setting for his novel: "Chin Yang Lee, himself a 'stranded Chinese' from Taiwan, might have been equipped to portray these exiled aristocrats with authenticity and deft satire; yet he felt obliged to use Chinatown, where the Taiwan refugees rarely settle, as the exotic setting of his story. Neither Lin nor Lee could speak with authority or truth about Chinatown life, partly because they were themselves never part of that life. Their own orientation made it difficult for them to distinguish between reality and stereotype." (Kim, *Asian American Literature*, p. 108) I disagree with this statement because the basic Confucian culture of the Taiwanese and the people of Chinatown is the same. Thus, although Lee might not have grown up in Chinatown, his representation of the Chinese people seems to be accurate. The problems reflected in the novel such as a shortage of women and widespread unemployment frustrated Chinese everywhere. In fact, we do get a picture of the outside world because two major female characters, Miss Tung and Helen Chao, do not live in Chinatown. Thus, it is inaccurate to say that the story takes place exclusively in Chinatown.

Flower Drum Song is the story of Wang Chi Yune and his two sons, Wang Ta and Wang San. Old Master Wang is a wealthy man who lives in a large house in Chinatown with his two sons and two servants. Although Wang Chi Yune is living in the States, he behaves as if he were living in China. This attitude governs his relationships with his family members and his servants. Old Master Wang refuses to adjust to his new surroundings. His first son goes to medical school because he can't find an acceptable job after graduation from college. His second son is a typical American teenager who likes hamburgers and baseball. However, the father insists on rearing his sons the traditional way. This is natural for the father. Gong points out, "For the Chinese, a primary part of their transmitted culture involves filial obligations. In the traditional Chinese world view, an individual sees his existence as part of an association of lives coming from father and ancestors continuing through his sons and descendants." (Gong, p. 74) The father is ever conscious of this fact.

Misunderstanding between the father and son provides the core of Lee's comedy. Marlom K. Hom, however, fails to see the humor in this situation: "one prominent immigrant writer, C.Y. Lee continues the simplistic stereotype of Chinese American Americans. In *Flower Drum Song* (New York, 1957), he characterizes the young boy Wang San as an 'American' youngster. Wang San behaves like an active American teenager. Because his behavior runs counter to the proper Chinese mannerism that his immigrant father treasures and expects of him, Wang San is seen as wild and undisciplined .... C.Y. Lee, sympathetic to the frustrations of the immigrant father, seems to condone such an interpretation of Wang San's American traits." (Hom, p. 31) It seems that Hom fails to see the clever use of dramatic irony. I think that Lee is actually more sympathetic to the younger generation or the son's point of view. As Gong points out, "The father/son relationship represents the most critical juncture in the erosion of a traditional Chinese value system and the emergence of a Chinese American character." (Gong, p. 74) Lee is not hostile to what "emerges" in this social pattern.

At this point it is interesting to examine some specific passages to see how Lee uses dramatic irony. The father often asks the younger son to recite for him because in traditional China that was the way people were educated. Thus, when the father asks Wang San to recite a chapter on arithmetic, Wang San "cleared his voice and repeated the American Declaration of Independence, twice this time. When he finished he shifted his legs restlessly and waited anxiously for his father to dismiss him." (*Flower Drum Song*, p. 41) The father, who cannot understand English, thinks that Wang San has just recited a chapter on arithmetic, but the reader knows what has really happened. Another example of dramatic irony occurs when the reader gets a glimpse into the father's thoughts. "Wang Chi-yang turned and walked hurriedly. He wondered what was happening to his two sons these days. One stayed out late, associated with foreign women and haunted public bars with a she-demon like this; the other talked a foreign tongue, ate with his hands, read strange picture books and tossed an ugly ball around every day. He must do something about his sons before they become too wild and foreign. He must talk to his wife's sister concerning Wang Ta and have her help in disciplining him; as for Wang San, perhaps he could deal with him alone. He would first order him to study Confucius and thus impart to him the fundamental Chinese morals ..." (*Flower Drum Song*, p. 65) The reader can smile at the father's "fears." "Foreign women," "public bars," "ugly ball," and "strange pictures" are all normal for an American teenager. This dramatic irony is effectively used. The reader does not laugh at the father and his different beliefs. Rather the reader's response is one of empathy as in a book like Jane Austen's *Emma*. Emma sometimes is not able to judge situations accurately. Yet Austen kindly leads the reader through her mistakes until Emma comes to a point of realization at the end. There is no indication that Lee is trying to portray the father as stupid. Rather Lee's objective is to reveal the cultural differences in a humorous way.

The main interest of the novel is in Wang Ta's relationships with women. There are three women in his life. The first is Miss Tung who is described as "the one who looks like a movie star." (*Flower Drum Song*, p. 24) (She is called Miss Tung because in Asia all women are called "Miss" or "Mrs." Their first names are rarely used.) Wang Ta's friend, Chang, warns him, "Likely she is just a playgirl." (*Flower Drum Song*, p. 28). However, Wang Ta is reluctant to believe his friend. The audience knows that she is not so much beautiful as artificial. She is not much of a cook, at any rate, for she invites Wang Ta to her apartment and "cook[s] him a five course dinner, with four of the courses ordered from the Express Kitchen on Broadway." (*Flower Drum Song*, p. 43) Although they are not on intimate terms, Miss Tung asks Wang Ta to change her sheets for her. To Wang Ta's surprise he finds a book with sexual illustrations hidden under the covers. Wang Ta's image of Miss Tung has been that of a pure and beautiful woman. He becomes suspicious when Miss Tung refers to a mysterious brother. Eventually, he discovers that in reality she is a prostitute. By the use of dramatic irony the reader discovers this fact earlier than Wang Ta, who leaves Miss Tung once he makes his discovery.

The second woman in Wang Ta's life is Miss Helen Chao, a forty-one-year-old seamstress. She is much older than Wang Ta, so he at first finds it comfortable to visit her. He "found a great deal of warmth in Miss Helen Chao's tiny apartment." (*Flower Drum Song*, p. 74) The apartment as well as the hospitality is warm and welcoming. Every time Wang Ta visits, Miss Chao prepares many of his favorite dishes. The food, furnishings, and friendship appeal to Wang Ta after a hard day at school. As a result his visits become more frequent.

Although Wang Ta regards Miss Chao as a friend, she has other designs. One night after an especially delicious meal and some strong Chinese wine, he feels drowsy. Helen suggests that he should rest on her bed. With Wang Ta on her bed, Helen grabs at her long awaited opportunity to seduce him. In his drunken state, he succumbs to her advances. (*Flower Drum Song*, p. 78) After the incident Wang Ta visits her often to have sex. However, he doesn't fall in love with her. One night she invites him to her birthday party. When he gets to the apartment he finds that he is the only guest. He is also surprised to find that her face is strangely red. Apparently, Helen just had a sandpaper treatment in an attempt to get rid of her pockmarks. Despite her appearance, Helen begs him to marry her: "'Love will grow, Ta,' she said, tightening her grip, 'Love will grow after marriage.'" Wang Ta bluntly replies, "I just don't love you. I don't think I shall ever be able to fall in love with you..." (*Flower Drum Song*, p. 91) The next day he reads in the newspaper that Helen was found dead on the beach, an apparent suicide.

Rather interestingly, although Miss Tung and Helen are very different, they both try to seduce Wang Ta. Wang Ta leaves Miss Tung because he feels that she is not the right type of person for him. He is offended by her many "brothers." With Helen he enjoys sex, but he feels that he can never love her. In fact he becomes ashamed of her. Wang Ta is frustrated because the Asian female population has always been low: "By 1890 Chinese women in the United States numbered only 3,868 in comparison to 103,620 men." (Fisher, p. 433) Although Lee's story takes place much later than 1890, Asian men have always outnumbered the women. The story could take place only after 1943 because Chinese women and children were not allowed to enter the United States until the Exclusion Act was repealed. (Fisher, p. 433)

The third woman in Wang Ta's life is May Li. It is interesting to note that she is called by her Chinese first name without a "Miss" in front of it. She is portrayed as a faithful daughter. She arrives in San Francisco with her father to find work and offers to carry her father's bag. "I can save energy for both of us if I carry your bag, father." (*Flower Drum Song*, p. 137) Together they beat their gongs, and May Li sings the Flower Drum Song on the streets of San Francisco to make money. They meet Wang Ta who invites them to his house for the night. The next day Wang Ta's father is persuaded to offer them jobs at his house.

May Li is not the typical gentle Chinese girl. She is young, outspoken, and sincere, and clearly expresses her desires and opinions. She refuses to work for Wang Ta's aunt because she would rather stay with her father. She is not afraid of the old female servant, Liu, who is a "shrew" when called names herself. Wang Ta falls in love with May Li and eventually asks her to marry him. Unlike Miss Tung and Miss Chao, May Li is portrayed as a simple, straightforward woman who provides a refreshing contrast to the other manipulative women. As Cinderella, May Li pleases the audience. Thus her forthcoming wedding to Wang Ta results in a happy ending.

Wang Ta's friend, Chang, is an interesting character who also illustrates Lee's relatively realistic intentions. Chang's function as a confidant seems to reflect the author's voice, rather like Maria Gostrey in James's *The Ambassadors*. Chang tells Wang Ta, "We cling to our old standards, ignorant of the fact that we are only a bunch of White Chinese, like the white Russians; we refuse to adjust ourselves to a new environment." (*Flower Drum Song*, p. 21) Chang adapts to his new environment. When Chang finds out that the only job he can land with a Ph.D. degree is as a grocery clerk, he adjusts to his new situation. Wang Ta admires Chang for his pragmatism and lack of bitterness: "It was unusual to find a person who was both cynical and optimistic. Undoubtedly Chang was such a strange character. Perhaps his attitude was a special product of this peculiar situation; perhaps it was a correct attitude, or even the only attitude a Chinese refugee should have in dealing with this situation if he wanted to be moderately happy." (*Flower Drum Song*, p. 118) Chang is indeed a pragmatist and a survivor.

The most dramatic scene in the novel (and play) also illustrates the realistic but ultimately upbeat or comic nature of Lee's narrative. Of the fourteen scenes in the two-act Broadway musical, the most memorable is the one in which May Li and her father are accused of stealing a gold clock. Liu Ma, the servant, hides the clock in May Li's bag. The father is upset when he finds the clock missing because it belonged to his late wife. He demands that May Li and her father's bags be searched. This is very humiliating, but they agree as they feel they have nothing to hide. To their surprise the clock tumbles out of May Li's bag. Everyone is shocked, believing that May Li stole the clock. Disgraced and angry, May Li and her father run out of the house. After Liu Ma's husband admits that Liu Ma is the real culprit, Wang Ta goes in search of May Li to ask her to marry him. Lee, who studied at the Yale School of Drama, incorporates several dramatic techniques into this episode. Like a stage director, Lee puts most of his characters on stage for this catastrophic scene which serves as a dramatic contrast to the happy ending. This scene heightens the effect of what follows just as comic relief heightens the tragic effect in a tragedy. In this scene there are misunderstandings and potential disaster, but the carefully planned resolution will be a happy one for characters and audience alike.

Lee's various portraits are realistic, sometimes even somber. Nonetheless, though there are tragic incidents in the novel such as Helen Chao's death, the general tone of the novel is relatively light. Lee's scheme illustrates the basically humorous and ironic truths of the Asian American existence. His narrative involves genuinely serious issues such as race and the assimilation of immigrants, but in *Flower Drum Song* these subjects are tempered with a gentle irony and humor.

Appreciative of Lee's wit and ironic humor, most readers approved. When the novel was adapted into a Broadway musical, the crowds applauded loudly. The 1961 Ross Hunter film proved a major success; millions of people all over the world laughed and sighed along with the characters. Lee went on to write several more novels: *Lover's Point* (1958), *Cripple Mah and the New Order* (1961), *The Virgin Market* (1964), *The Land of the Golden Mountain* (1967), among others. Of these later books, however, only *Lover's Point* approaches *Flower Drum Song* as a work of literature.

Lover's Point is not a comedy. It is a serious and sincere treatment of a man's love for a prostitute. Emotions are portrayed with sufficient honesty that some critics believe the story belongs in the romantic tradition: "Unlike most Chinatown authors whose main concern is the realistic description of their ethnic experiences, the majority of writers in this literary group tend to use passion in their works; they enthusiastically admire sensuality, emotion, and nature. They seem Oriental-American Byrons in the 20th century." (Han, p. 241) Indeed, Han thinks that "the heroes and heroines of [*Lover's Point*] endeavor to guide their lives through passion rather than reason. They respect the pleasure of sensory gratification, believing that only human sexual orgasm will lead them to spiritual satisfaction." (Han, p. 241) This strong observation is an exaggeration, however. If the above were true, Lee's novel would focus on sex like Jackie Collins' novels. The novel's compassion and pathos are of a quite different order. Joseph Conrad once said, "A writer without interest or sympathy for the foibles of his fellow man is not conceivable as a writer." (Burnett, p. 16) Lee's portrayal of the prostitute and the lonely Chinese is full of such compassionate understanding. Lee's aim here is to paint a picture with sufficient pathos and sympathy for the reader to identify with the characters.

The language and title of Lee's novel suggest his realistic intentions. All the characters talk as if they were speaking in Chinese. As Han points out, "even though the speech is written in grammatically acceptable English, it sounds like

Chinese and reflects Chinese language features." (Han, p. 153)
For example, Old Chao says, "Sometimes he and his wife like
to ask me questions about China. I worried about his heart, so
I talked about Chinese heart." (*Lover's Point*, p. 149) Another
character, Miss Chung, cries, "Ooo television! Picture come in
from the window! I know, I know. I saw it in Hong Kong.
They talked the foreign talk. I didn't understand much."
(*Lover's Point*, p. 128) The characters do not speak English
correctly, but this is a precise reproduction of how some
Chinese speak English. The narration, of course, is in excellent English, as when we are led into Chiang's thoughts: "The
water dropping into the assorted bowls made pleasant noise
that faintly resembled the Hindu music Chiang had heard in
Bombay seven years ago." (*Lover's Point*, p. 16) The images
are distinctly Chinese and together with the spoken language
appropriately represent the characters in the story. The
realistic content of Lee's second novel is also suggested by its
title, *Lover's Point*, a secluded parking spot for lovers in
Orange Grove. Unlike *Flower Drum Song*, this title evokes a
real place. Indeed, the two titles evoke different worlds.
Whereas *Flower Drum Song* suggests an imaginary and pretty
world that is definitely Asian, *Lover's Point* suggests a passion-
ate and universal fictional world. These different associations
give us a clue to the essential difference between Lee's two best
works. The first is a comic novel, the second a psychological
novel.

The phrase "psychological novel" has been used to refer to a
wide range of works including those by James, Woolf, and
Joyce. Surmelian's definition fits the framework of *Lover's
Point*: "We might say the modern novel, and particularly the
psychological novel, is the history and anatomy of a complex
emotion. The writer characterizes his people and brings them
to life through a minute analysis or dramatization of their
feelings and ideas. The definition of the emotion means the
definition of the situation in which one or more people are
involved. We know then what the problem is. It is not a
purely private problem, and unless the universal is implied in
the particular, we do not have a work of art. Like the scientist,
the fiction writer deduces general laws from the particular

cases before him." (Surmelian, p. 92) The complex emotion defined here can be compared to Chiang's strong love for Aika, the underlying force that unites Lee's book. Moments of anger, suspicion, and sympathy complicate and define this central love relationship.

Chiang's story is sometimes told from the point of view of a detached observer, but it is primarily told from his own perspective. By means of the limited third person point of view Lee concentrates on Chiang's thoughts. This viewpoint keeps the focus from drifting away toward other characters, which would diminish our sense of Chiang's emotional tension. Chiang's moments of indecision and self-scrutiny provide the main conflict in the novel. Faulkner says that "the problems of the human heart in conflict with itself alone can make good writing because only that is worth writing about, worth the agony and the sweat." (Rockwell, p. 119) Lee's intense psychological story explores such "problems" even as it offers a compelling portrait of Chiang's spiritual life. The following passage is representative: "[Chiang] finally came to the conclusion that religion, philosophy, psychology, Confucius, Laotze, etc. were only the skill of the different holds of a wrestler, the fundamental strength of the man must be built in the rearing. Understanding this he suddenly felt a strong compassion for the sinners, the criminals, the cynics, the suicides, for they were only the victims of the villain personality, which defeated the hero personality with brutal force; they were the ones who were totally beyond their own control. When he thought of this he somehow felt there was no hatred in him" (*Lover's Point*, p. 93) From this passage we learn that Chiang is a compassionate person with a mature understanding of others. Such passages prepare us to care about Chiang's subsequent turmoil.

Chiang's inner conflict is the novel's center. Throughout the story, the reader gets deeper and deeper insights into Chiang's thoughts. It is evident that Chiang thinks constantly of Aika, and the fact that she sees other men torments him. He is especially jealous of a man named Larson: "For the next week he tried not to think of Aika and Lieutenant Larson: he drove to Lover's Point in Pacific Grove several times to watch the ocean, to meditate and plan his future .... He enjoyed his thought and the beauty of nature until he saw a young couple climbing rocks at Lover's Point .... It was then Chiang couldn't stay there anymore, for they reminded him of Aika and Lieutenant Larson making love, and the nameless pain began to gnaw at him again." (*Lover's Point*, pp. 59-60) Even in his room Chiang cannot escape thinking about Aika. "After he had fixed the calendar he returned to his bed but he couldn't relax any more. The nude girl had reminded him of Aika, now she returned to his mind, and peace and relaxation flew out of the window." (*Lover's Point*, p. 79) These sharp reminders pierce his thoughts while his indecision torments him. "To his surprise the disturbance, which had come like a slow pain, gradually disappeared. He began to analyze why the meeting with Aika had caused him such a bad day. Was it because he had been torn between his determination not to see her and a strong desire to see her again? There must have been a battle raging furiously in his subconscious mind. His reasoning power must have fought a desperate defensive war against his emotions." (*Lover's Point*, p. 247) Such feelings and perceptions are the novel's driving forces as the different faces of love attack Chiang's soul.

The beginning and the ending of the novel occur at the same place, the Tokyo Garden Restaurant. On the novel's first page, we are told, "The service at Tokyo Garden was slow, but the tempura, the sushi, and sukiyaki served there were excellent, and the Japanese waitress was another great attraction." (*Lover's Point*, p. 1) This waitress is Aika, whom Chiang meets here at the beginning of the novel. Chiang's life as a language instructor is very lonely; his insufficient paycheck allows one good meal at the Tokyo Garden on Saturday nights and a rented room. One night Aika asks him for a ride and they end up in his apartment. He finds out that she is a prostitute but nevertheless develops a strong passion and love for her. This love will survive her other affairs, her engagement to another man, and even her later suicide attempt.

Lee's treatment of Chiang's strong love is full of compassion. Although Han states that "some knowledge of Oriental ethics would help the reader of C. Y. Lee's *Lover's Point* understand the moral conflict inherent in the differences between the Western and Eastern concepts of love and marriage" (Han, p. 6), I don't find any conflict here because Chiang and Aika's love is not bound by cultural chains. Chiang is not restricted by an Asian code of values which frowns upon falling in love with a prostitute. Nor is Chiang concerned about saving face; he is more concerned with saving Aika. His love is strong and pure, the sort of love understandable to readers of all cultures and universally appealing. Although Aika admits to being a prostitute, Chiang persists in asking her to marry him. Most readers are glad at the end of the story when Aika finally seems happy to see Chiang sitting at his table ordering his usual meal.

After Chiang loses his job he moves to San Francisco where he works for a wealthy Chinese merchant, Mr. Yee, a middle-aged man who lives with his mother. Aika eventually comes to ask Chiang for help. He finds her a job as a nurse for Mr. Yee's mother. A relationship develops between Aika and Mr. Yee, who asks Aika to marry him although she is pregnant with another man's child. Chiang believes that he is the father and tells Mr. Yee. Mr. Yee tries to give Chiang $5000 to keep this secret. Despite the fact that Chiang has quit working for Mr. Yee, Chiang returns the money. When the baby is born, however, it turns out to be Amerasian. This fact makes Mr. Yee break his engagement to Aika, for he cannot claim the baby as his own. At this point Aika attempts suicide but fails.

The attempted suicide culminates Aika's disappointments. One incident after another creates more and more stress. Aika relates to Chiang how she ended up divorced because her husband's mother strongly opposed their interracial marriage. After her divorce Aika became a waitress and prostitute to feed her two children. Later she fell in love with Lieutenant Larson, but he disappeared after she told him that she was a prostitute. For Aika, death seems the only possible resolution to her trials.

Lee is very sympathetic toward such despair. He narrates another incident that parallels Chiang and Aika's situation. A stranger named Ah Hing dies alone in a hospital. The only person who befriends him is a prostitute. "Ah Hing had probably come to this country fifteen or twenty years ago, when he was a young man of perhaps thirty, speaking very little English. He had worked hard and supported his family of six ... In the meantime he wanted to be with his family. He had tried to get them moved but failed. He worked harder, hoping to retire earlier, so that he could see his family sooner. But he contracted T.B." (*Lover's Point*, p. 83) After Ah Hing dies in the hospital, Chiang reflects on this stranger. "The more he thought of Ah Hing the more identical their lives seemed to be. The only difference was that he had more education than Ah Hing and he was luckier." (*Lover's Point*, p. 83) These comments seem to embody Lee's point of view.

Lover's Point is an accurate treatment of the suffering of Chinese Americans. As one of the character states, "That is the problem of the whole Chinese population in America -loneliness ... Just take a look at the Chinese walking on Grant Avenue, I mean the Chinese from China, their lonely looks break your heart." (*Lover's Point*, p. 150) The novel focuses on hunger, whether it is for food, companionship, or sex. All the characters seem to be longing for something: Aiki for a man whom she loves to return her love, Chiang for Aiki's love, Mr. Yee for a wife and children, and Mr. Yee's mother for grandchildren. The several scenes involving sex and food point up this theme. In fact, as a friend of Chiang's says, "Food and sex are actually one subject. Even Confucius, our greatest sage, did not separate them." (*Lover's Point*, p. 201) The descriptions of love and food make the reader see, touch, hear, and smell the several scenes, and they are almost always lonely ones.

At the end of the novel Chiang finds that "Aika's image came back to his mind vividly now, standing on the dark porch of Mr. Tanaka's two story house, holding the railing with a hand like a very tired woman, frail and lonely .... The desolate image suddenly aroused in him a deep compassion that almost made his eyes moisten. He lay on the beach till the sun had sunk behind the water, setting half the ocean aflame." (*Lover's Point* p. 248) Chiang's anger and jealousy seem to disappear at that moment. Instead a feeling of compassion overcomes him. Revelation follows compassion, as Chiang is led to return to the scene where he met Aika. There he encounters his love once again. "Aika, wearing a colorful kimono, came out of the kitchen with a tray of food. Under the bright light she looked older; about five years older. Her walk was less energetic and the swing of her hips, which had been a great attraction at Tokyo Garden more than a year ago, was half-hearted now. Everything about her showed the wear and tear of the part year, a ruthless and long year ... How it had changed her! ... 'Your usual, Mr Chiang?' she asked softly. 'Yes, my usual,' Chiang said, smiling." (*Lover's Point*, pp. 248-249) Chiang's smile and Aika's subsequent tears of joy suggest the possibility of a reconciliation. Given what has passed between Chiang and Aika, it seems appropriate to have a simple and relatively happy ending. Although unresolved, this last scene offers the persuasive promise of such an ending.

In sum, Lee is one of the best Asian American writers. In *Flower Drum Song* his ability to combine ancient literary princi- ples with contemporary Asian American materials allows him to reach the general American audience. In *Lover's Point* the realistic and compassionate depiction of his characters is also successful. In these two novels Lee demonstrates his ability to use sophisticated techniques, comic as well as psychological. With skillful artistry, creative humor, and psychological realism, Lee has painted two contrasting but equally valid pictures of the Asian American experience.

Chapter Three

Kim Yong Ik: Short Story Writer

The first group of Asian American writers usually drew upon their experiences in their own countries as subject matter. The first group also came to the United States as young men, their minds and characters firmly rooted in their own cultures. Kim Yong Ik is an example of the early Asian American writer: he came to the United States in 1948 when he was twenty-eight-years-old and presently teaches at Duquesne University in Pittsburgh, Pennsylvania. The author of juvenile novels such as *The Happy Days, Diving Gourd,* and *Moons of Korea,* as well as several collections of short stories, Kim draws upon his memories of the small quiet village in the southern tip of the Korean peninsula where he grew up.

Chungmu, known as Tongyong at the time, was a small seaport village, with the smell of fresh fish from the clear blue waters, narrow cobblestone streets dividing the tile and thatched roof houses, and round green hills overlooking the sea. Although quiet and graceful like an Asian painting outlined with light black strokes on a scroll, the village contained its share of broken hearts, wounded pride, and shattered dreams. Memories of falling snow and footsteps, bright harvests, lonely nightboats carrying their load of humanity, and a crowded marketplace exchanging pride for money provide images that Kim recreates in his stories.

Four hundred years ago Kim Yong Ik's ancestors came to live in Chungmu. His family belonged to the yangban class, the upper class in Korea. Kim Yong Ik had a happy childhood. His family consisted of his father, mother, older brother, and older sister. He attended the village elementary and high schools, then went to Aoyama Gakuin College in Tokyo from 1939 to 1943. At that time Korea was annexed to

Japan and many Koreans went to Japan for higher education.
Upon graduation he taught English in secondary schools and
colleges until the end of World War II. In 1948 he left Korea
to pursue his ambition to become a writer. He left behind his
wife, whom his parents had arranged for him to marry, and
his three children.

Kim spent the next ten years in the United States attending
various universities such as Florida Southern College, the
University of Kentucky, and the Writer's Workshop at the
University of Iowa.   His roommate at Florida Southern
College told him, "If I were you, I wouldn't waste time in this
country. I'll give you five hundred dollars if you publish one
book in America. Breaking into that racket is nearly impossible even for an American writer who has mastered his own
language." (*Writer*, p. 28) This, however, did not deter Kim
from his writing. "In America, I wanted to write so much that I
refused to accept the fact that my English was far from being
adequate to write a novel. I put in three hours early every
morning writing a book." (*Writer*, p. 28) Kim enrolled at the
University of Iowa and kept on writing. He wrote and rewrote
constantly. He read and reread. He revised and revised.
However, he continued to receive rejection slips. "As days and
seasons passed, I became desperate. I read and wrote harder
than before ... At night, I stayed up late writing. Word got
around that the Korean liked to sleep with his light on."
(*Writer*, p. 29) He felt discouraged. "I wanted to have one
story accepted. I was beginning to feel that perhaps this would
never happen. I had only my many rejection slips to contem-
plate — after so many years of labor." (*Writer*, p. 29)

Nonetheless, word by word, sentence by sentence, story by
story, Kim built up his success. Kim's first story, "The
Wedding Shoes," was finally accepted by *Harper's Bazaar*. After
that his stories were accepted by *Mademoiselle*, *Botteghe Oscure*,
and *The New Yorker*, and in 1958 "From Below the Bridge" was
cited in Martha Foley's *Best American Short Stories*. Kim Yong
Ik is now the only Korean American who publishes frequently
in quality magazines such as *The New Yorker*, *Mademoiselle*, and
Harper's Bazaar. Kim's dedication to the short story form is no
accident, for like other Koreans of his time he believed that

the story was the supreme artistic creation. In Korea until the 1970's the short story rather than the novel occupied a distinguished position. "An excellent short story will receive much critical applause while a number of popular novels go unnoticed simply because they are written for lowbrows." (Yu Jung Ho, p. ix) Kim's artistic aspirations dictated his choice of genre, then, and in the late 1950's he accomplished his dream to become the first Korean to publish a short story in English.

Review and assessment of Kim's work might well begin with "From Here You Can See the Moon" (1963), because the story is about Kim's return to his village after many years abroad and thus provides an intimate portrait of the author's background and character. In this story Kim uses the first-person point of view, which allows for increased emotional impact and intensifies the reader's response. As Leon Surmelian points out about Edgar Allan Poe's stories, " A strong emotional experience is told best by the person who had it, it can be pitched at a higher level and read like a confession torn from the heart. Poe needed the first person for his emotion-charged poetic prose." (Surmelian, p. 67) Like Poe, Kim uses the first person to help the reader identify with an otherwise foreign experience. Like many of Kim's stories, this piece fulfills Poe's famous definition of the short story by producing a strong, single effect. In this case the overall effect is one of emotional pain. Many of Kim's stories are about painful memories. The sharp and precise descriptions are like the Emily Dickinson poems that define qualities of pain. Indeed, a Kim Yong Ik short story seems to be a dramatization of the degrees of emotional pain. The reader becomes aware of the intensity as the story cuts into his or her sensibilities.

Like Dickinson's, Kim's style is forceful and direct but rhetorically adept. For example, in "I Felt a Funeral in My Brain" Dickinson describes her mind as going numb in an extremity of pain. Toward this end she often uses synecdoche, as in "And Being, but an Ear." Earlier in the same poem she uses metonymy: "I felt a Funeral in my Brain/ And Mourners to and fro, Kept treading—treading ..." In this example "Brain" is treated as a place. Kim Yong Ik also frequently uses synecdoche. In "From Here You Can See the Moon" he writes, "No face I knew; nor did any face know me." It is interesting to note that synecdoche is common in the Korean language. Therefore, "No face I knew; nor did any face know me" is a literal translation. Such translations are intended to make the character's speech more authentic. The narrator is Korean, so of course he should speak like a Korean.

As mentioned above, Dickinson frequently wrote about states of mind. Indeed, her best poetry deals with qualities of emotional pain. In "After great pain, a formal feeling comes" various parts of the body are personified. "The Nerves sit ceremonious, like Tombs—/ The stiff Heart questions was it He, that bore/ And Yesterday, or Centuries before? The Feet, mechanical, go round—/ "This technique allows the reader to feel and to understand the intensity of the pain. Again, the following lines from another poem illustrate a state of pain: "There is a pain—so utter,/ It swallows substance up - / Then covers the Abyss with Trance - / So Memory can step / Around—across—upon it—/ As one within a Swoon—/ Goes safely—where an open eye—/ Would drop Him—Bone by Bone." In this example one notes the extensive use of personification. "Memory" is capitalized like "Nerves" and "Tombs" in the previous illustration. This unusual technique is quite effective in describing the writer's or persona's state of mind. Just as Dickinson's egocentric concentration is one of her strengths, so Kim's egocentric topics and style are his strengths. Both Dickinson and Kim also use interesting word associations to communicate their points. Dickinson writes: "Our lives are Swiss—So Swiss, so Cool—" The use of "Swiss" as a metaphor to describe "lives" is a unique association. Similarly Kim writes: "When we were as young as green pepper days." "Green pepper days" is an especially appropriate association for Kim because he walked past vegetable fields everyday when he was growing up.

In analyzing Kim's style, we see that it is simple yet graceful. "From Here You Can See the Moon" reminds me of a soprano coloratura's voice ending in a strikingly high note. The sentences are usually short, personification is common, and the images are precise even in longer passages ("the long-forgotten song of green frogs sighing in the rice fields and the high-low notes I used to make on my willow whistle crowded into my fears, and my feet quickened toward home" ["From Here You Can See the Moon" p. 86]). Kim's words are carefully selected and each image is carved precisely. His words seem to be polished with a wet pebble. Yet the style also conveys real emotion. As the boat approaches his hometown, the narrator is excited about coming home: "How many years I had longed to come home by the day boat to see the dock crowded with my hometown people! But in the early years, I always came by nightboat, after having visited my brother in Pusan. From him I had asked and received money for painting materials. Returning on the nightboat, I could come home without being asked, 'What have you got there? I wish I had a brother like you have. You don't have to do anything but just paint, paint as you please eh?" ("From Here You Can See the Moon," p. 75) This passage gives the reader a clear understanding of the narrator's feelings as he approaches his hometown. As Surmelian suggests, "The style is a true measure of the man. It is always in character, the authentic idiom of the writer himself." (Surmelian, p. 237) So it is in the selection above, in which Kim skillfully combines the authentic Korean voice with the character's emotional state.

What makes Kim's stories unusually authentic is the extensive and realistic use of local color. Thus we see vividly the speech, mannerisms, inner thoughts, and general eccentricities of the local people. The minor characters in "From Here You Can See the Moon" add such color and reflect the people of Chungmu at that time: the painted woman (a Korean Moll Flanders), the boatman, an old woman seller of seaweed and squid, and the two shoeshine boys represent the people who try to make a living on a nightboat. Images of Chungmu such as the seaweed, shoeshine boys, green frogs, and crowded small boats enhance the sense of persuasive realistic detail. The characters are not individualized; rather they are called "a painted woman," "a boy," etc. But this is the way people are called in Korea. Every boy is called "a boy," and an older woman is usually called "an aunt." Thus the portrayal is not intended to be stereotypical but realistic. In addition the use of "won" Korean currency is authentic and the way the characters interact is typically Korean. When Kim Yong Ik offers to buy food, the boys refuse because they want to work for their money. After eating their hard-earned food, the boys cry. This detail shows that Kim Yong Ik wanted to portray the dignity of even the shoeshine boys. The painter in the story is judged in part by his outward appearance. Although he is a famous painter, he wears only relief clothes. Thus, he doesn't get any respect from the boatman and others, who mistake him for a person with no money. However, when he tells them that his brother is the governor, "the same hand that had grabbed me rose to salute me." The detail of the relief clothes is interesting because in real life Kim Yong Ik always wears the worst clothes. Once he was stopped on a street at night in Pittsburgh because the police thought he was a bum.

The conflict in the story is internal and concerns what the narrator should feel as a brother as opposed to the chagrin he really feels because after all these years he still cannot outshine his brother. The narrator is constantly reminded of his brother's status as the governor. He hopes that his own success as a painter in the United States will finally convince his father of his own worth. He wants to show his father "the picture of myself and 'Angry Owl,' far too bright in reproduction. I would show my father this. This would top the citations, certifications, diplomas which my brother had been awarded since early school days. I could still see my brother run into the yard and bring one of those papers. My father proudly would paste it beside his other award papers on the mud wall of our house. My father used to blush as some visitor would praise them, 'He is the town genius. Let him do whatever he wants to. Make your younger son work on the farm.'" ("From Here You Can See the Moon," p. 76) As this passage suggests, Kim Yong Ik grew up in his brother's shadow.

Kim's father was traditional and strict. He was not sensitive to the needs of his younger son. Thus, when Kim Yong Ik one day pasted his best calligraphy over his brother's award papers, his father ordered him to erase his writing. In this story Kim's character undergoes the same experience—his father beats him and makes him "wipe off each stroke of my writing ....The hot blood still coursed through my cheek with the memory." ("From Here You Can See the Moon," p. 77) Whether this incident really happened to Kim is hard to prove, though family members allude to it. However, Kim Yong Ik did feel jealousy towards his brother, who was physically much taller, better looking, smarter, and the father's favorite. Indeed, Kim has said that his desire to be like his brother kept him writing and eventually brought him success. It is interesting to note that his brother, Kim Yong Shik, later served as Foreign Minister and as ambassador to ten countries. Kim Yong Shik also served as the first chairman of the Seoul Olympic Organizing Committee.

The climax of the story comes when Kim returns home and is greeted warmly by his father. Kim looks into the room with the wall where so often he has seen all his brother's awards posted. He sees that his father has kept his poem "From Here You Can See the Moon" on the center of the wall. Thus, after all the years of bitterness and resentment, he realizes that his father is proud of him. The moment of revelation almost leads him to break down and cry: "fearing I might wail loud as the whistle of the midnight boat, I ran ahead into the house." ("From Here You Can See the Moon," p. 89) It is a highly emotional and moving ending to the story, a final revelation that seems to fit Joyce's conception of the short story as epiphany.

"From Here You Can See the Moon" tells us much about Kim's origins, but "The Wedding Shoes" (1958) was Kim's first important success. Kim has told us a great deal about the composition of this story: "I was feeling so dejected that I went out and spent nearly all my remaining money on a record player. At least I could have music. Then I borrowed a record of Beethoven's 'Emperor's Concerto' from the library and played it over and over all that day, not even stopping to eat.... As I sat listening and watching the falling snow, I had a strange fantasy. I imagined I saw a pair of Korean wedding shoes walking away from me in the snow. I followed the shoes in my mind, but I was always behind the figure who wore them, watching the back of the silk brocade shoes and the white muslin socks with a canoe-shaped line around the feet ...

I thought that only I could see the elusive owner of these
shoes, then I could write a real story." (*Writer*, p. 28) That day
was Christmas day. The story Kim started writing was "The
Wedding Shoes." Earlier in the day he had gone to a butcher
with only a few coins; the butcher gave him a generous piece
of meat and wished him a Merry Christmas. In the story, the
butcher appears as a kind man. Thus, Kim often reworked his
life in his lonely room. However, wherever there was an
empty seat in a library, or paper and a pen, or a Korean-
English dictionary, Kim felt happy despite his desperation and
loneliness.

"The Wedding Shoes" is about rejected love. The central
character is the butcher's son who falls in love with his neighbor's daughter, the shoemaker's daughter. Although the
butcher and the shoemaker are neighbors, they belong to
different classes. Generally speaking the butchers in Korea
are thought to be of the lowest class. Thus when the butcher's
son asks the shoemaker's daughter to marry him, the shoemaker rejects him. Although less wealthy than the butcher, the
shoemaker still clings to his pride and refuses to let his daughter marry Sangdo, the butcher's son. It is ironic that the
shoemaker lets his daughter work as a maid to help pay off
some of his debts but refuses to allow her to marry Sangdo.

As I will argue more fully in a moment, the overall structure
of the story recalls Aristotle's definition of tragedy. It is the
father's pride that causes his eventual sadness and death. The
father's stubbornness also prevents his daughter and Sangdo
from fulfilling their love for each other. Like a Korean
version of *Romeo and Juliet*, the story is therefore about
frustrated love. Here the lovers do not die, however; rather,
it is the girl's father who dies after losing all his money. The
story is nonetheless told from Sangdo's point of view, and the
main tragedy in the story involves Sangdo's suffering.

We might also recall that Aristotle praised metaphor as "the
greatest thing by far" among the writer's techniques. Kim's
use of metaphor is but one of many successful devices in this
story. Kim's very title, "The Wedding Shoes," serves as a
metaphor for the story's principal theme. The wedding shoes
stand for love and rejection; they stand for a tradition of

handmade quality that no longer exists in modern society; and they also represent an old man's refusal to adapt to the modern world. The shoes are therefore a major symbol. In explaining the use of symbols, Norman Friedman states, "Basically it refers to the way in which experience can have significance and can mean anything from a central or repeated image or character or situation which appears to carry the weight of special value, to the way in which the work itself can embody and organize the author's vision and reveal insights into the human condition." (Friedman, p. 56) Kim uses his symbol to remind the reader of his tragic vision. In the first sentence the "silk brocade shoes" are introduced, while the last words of the last sentence in the story are "silk brocade shoes." The first and last scenes of the story take place at the shoe stand. Thus the wedding shoes serve as the story's controlling image. As Surmelian argues, "What makes the metaphor makes also the plot, and the structure and texture of a story." (Surmelian, p. 230) The wedding shoes are related to the plot because the story is about the shoemaker's daughter's marriage which never takes place. The shoes also connect the past to the present, for they remind the narrator of his painful memories. Thematically, the shoes are also used to show that the world no longer cares for beautifully made wedding shoes. Sangdo realizes this: "Then I would grow aware of the noises of the market and walk with the crowd: every kind of shoes—straw shoes, hob-nailed shoes. All looked so heavy." ("The Wedding Shoes," p. 40) Kim's story mirrors reality here, for people no longer dress in Korean clothes; with the Korean War western influence permeates every aspect of Korean society. Thus the wedding shoes represent several important threads in Kim's story.

In this story Kim Yong Ik also uses rhetorical techniques such as synecdoche and repetition to embody his theme. "His fists held bitterness" and "Mouth refused proposal" are examples of the former. Unlike his use of synecdoche in "From Here You Can See the Moon," such as "No face I knew, nor did any face know me," the two examples above are not translations. Kim invented these images that effectively advance the meaning of the story. Repetition also figures prominently, as in this passage: "People poured into the city; with no invitation, they were guests of no one, but guests of the dusty street; road guests, they called themselves." ("The Wedding Shoes" p. 38) The repetition of "guests" connects with the image of the wedding shoes by reinforcing the contrast between past and present. As the wedding shoes become outdated, so do traditional weddings filled with many guests. Thus, "no invitation" and "guests of no one" underline this contrast. Kim also likes to repeat independent clauses. "Perhaps it was the pleasantly chilly autumn wind through the red, dusky maple; perhaps it was the color of the sky; perhaps it was the echoes of my heart to others' marriage talks; perhaps the thread of that colorful day might have moved my long-timed feet toward that house." ("The Wedding Shoes," p. 27) The repetition of the word "perhaps" effectively underlines the narrator's insecurity and uncertainty.

Kim uses a lot of images that are uniquely Korean and add a special local color. For example, when Sangdo overhears his marriage proposal being rejected by the shoemaker, "The words came to [him] like round flower bowls falling one on another." ("The Wedding Shoes," p. 36) Elsewhere in the story, "Word got around as quickly as the light of the kerosene lamps after sunset in the village homes." ("The Wedding Shoes," p. 34) Like the Korean language in general, Kim uses distance metaphorically as time: "The wedding day he mentioned seemed remote, far beyond many mountains." ("The Wedding Shoes," p. 34) These examples illustrate Kim's conscious effort to adapt Korean linguistic features to English: "I tried to capture the rhythm of my own language in English writing and tried not to take a chance of any misunderstanding by putting everything in concrete terms. Whenever I found it difficult to describe a certain scene, I had my usual temptation to delete it. But by this time I knew better than to glide over any scene or word that belonged in my work; more often than not, the thorny word or passage that does pose a language problem is the one that breathes pulsating life into the story." (*Writer* p. 29) This passage explains several features of Kim's text: the dialogue in which his characters use Korean expressions rather than perfect English; the many sentences that consist of independent clauses joined together by conjunctions (the rhythm of the Korean language is often like that of a freight train); the many images that may seem strange to the western reader because some of them are literally translated from Korean.

Examples of the latter are especially interesting. "Spring did come to Pusan, after winter, with soft peppery winds from the Japan Sea. It blew the skirts of the city girls in every direction—but I did not chase the spring wind with city girls." ("The Wedding Shoes," p. 38) The skirts not only indicate the movement of the wind; literally translated the passage means that Sangdo did not have any love affairs with girls who were willing. "Charging sky-high prices for behind the time shoes! Old man, you are asleep, scratching another's leg instead of your own itching one." ("The Wedding Shoes," p. 39) The words "scratching another's legs" mean that by charging high prices the shoemaker is losing his business to others. The image points up the shoemaker's tragic inability to adjust to changing times. The shoemaker cannot face the reality that his people no longer care to spend a lot of money for the brocade shoes. Before the Korean War in 1950 the shoemaker held a high position and his shoes were in great demand. The traditional shoes were handmade and took a long time to finish. In the old days it was the pride of every bride to wear these delicately made shoes, which were individually ordered and considered an art form. However, after the Korean War such luxuries lost their appeal and these shoes were no longer in demand. Thus, the shoemakers became poor like the shoemaker in Kim's story.

A final example of Kim's technique is his use of contrasts, perhaps suggested by his happy childhood and positive expectations followed by disappointment and rejection. Examples include the contrast between the two families and their social status, the reversal of their economic situation, social customs before and after the war, and traditional and modern shoes. The most significant contrast involves Sangdo's painful memories and his renewed efforts to cope with life at the end of the story. Sangdo's story begins and ends at the same place, the empty shoe stand at the marketplace. "Outside the market, the wind blew up snow. I brought the umbrella back to a half-open position ..." The conflict is resolved in Sangdo's mind as he brings the umbrella to a "half-open position." This indicates Sangdo's desire to compromise and to address his conflicts in a more positive way.

Beyond the individual techniques that characterize "The Wedding Day," I would note the impressionistic quality to Kim's story. As in Renoir's nineteenth-century paintings, the story's overall effect is based on artistic presentation rather than the reproduction of actual events. Local color and the realistic portrayal of character are important, but the overall structure is impressionistic. Kim's story again seems to fit Poe's definition of the short story, for the total effect is what comes across most strongly. The story's images unfold as in an impressionistic painting; memories overlap and are repeated in blurry yet lingering images. According to the usual definition of Impressionism, "The object of the impressionist ... is to present material not as it is to the objective observer but as it is seen or felt to be by the impressionist or a character in a single passing moment. The impressionistic writer employs highly selective details, the 'brush strokes' of sense-data that can suggest impressions." (Holman and Harmon, p. 253) So it is in Kim's fine story.

As I suggested earlier, the characters' reversals in fortune recall Aristotle's *Poetics*, chapter 13. As Aristotle states, "... the cause of [the protagonist's downfall] must lie not in any depravity, but in some great fault on his part." (Aristotle, p. 2325) The concept of pride is what drives the entire plot of "The Wedding Shoes." Almost all the main characters show some evidence of self-pride. The shoemaker's wife, although one feels she is proud also, seems to have the least amount of destructive pride. She goes to the butcher's and accepts the extra leather for her husband's shoes and when Sangdo proposes she is pleased. Her pride is not so overwhelming that it blinds her to the realities that surround her, as it does her husband. For Sangdo, pride is what prevents him from approaching the shoemaker's family again after they reject his proposal. Perhaps this pride mixed with anger is what drives him to almost commit murder when he hears the shoemaker's insults through the window. More obviously, pride dominates the personality of the shoemaker. It is pride that causes him to drink nights after the butcher has had much business. It is pride that keeps his aging business alive in his own eyes, though he is unable to lower prices or modernize in any way. Ultimately, it is pride that causes him to reject Sangdo's proposal, for the shoemaker thinks a butcher's son is beneath the daughter of a shoemaker and he is also insulted that Sangdo fails to get a matchmaker to make his proposal. Finally, the shoemaker drives himself to an early death. He will not give up his craft, nor change his business in any way to keep up with the times. Pride therefore drives him to complete misery.

Although the shoemaker is not in the same category as Greek or Shakespearean royalty, Aristotle's tragic flaw seems to exist in all men. Interestingly, Aristotle says that "Euripides .... is seen to be nevertheless the most tragic certainly of the dramatists." (Aristotle, p. 2325) Many critics note that Euripides has greatly influenced modern literature: "Remove Euripides and the modern theatre ceases to exist." (Oates and O'Neill, p. xxxii) As Oates and O'Neill point out, "His [Euripides'] greatest claims to fame ... rest on his superb studies of human problems considered on the human level, his penetrating psychological analyses of the dramatic possibilities of an individual scene, and his ability by means of dramatic innovations to reinterpret the traditional legends upon which all the dramatists relied for their material." (Oates and O'Neill, p. xxxi) Kim seems to be following Euripides in his portrayal of human weaknesses.

Pride is the principal motive that allows Kim to create a causal sequence of actions leading to a tragic end. The result is a story with Aristotelian unity, for, as Friedman remarks, "Aristotle counsels against the use in tragedy of a deus ex machina, an incident which resolves the action but which does not follow from what went before." (Friedman, p. 65) This story is unified in all ways. The events leading to the rejection are revealed by means of flashback. The story begins and ends in the present, with past events told step by step via flashbacks. Thus the reader understands the causal sequence that creates the narrator's inner conflict, and the structure as well as the effect of the story seems tragic.

Tragic themes have always been a part of Korean literature. However, tragedy as a genre in the western use of the word has not existed in Korea, where there has been no attempt to define tragedy as a literary form. Korean tragic stories have not been shaped by structural elements such as hamartia, catastrophe, catharsis, and hubris, nor have they been governed by a logical progression of events leading to unity of action. I would add that it is not surprising that Korean literature is filled with sad themes as Korean history is filled with wars and foreign occupations. In 1910 Japan annexed Korea, bringing about hardship and suppression. From 1914 to 1947 Japan wanted a complete Japanization of Korea, which meant no Korean literature. After liberation from Japan, Koreans endured three more years of hardship during the Korean War. Kim grew up during these dark times. He left Korea shortly after the end of World War II to study in the United States. For ten years he studied western literature and writing. He studied the western use of metaphor with great interest. Although metaphor has existed in both western and oriental literature, its use has not been the same. Michelle Yeh points out that "whereas metaphor is the figure par excellence in western poetics, it never attains quite the same status in Chinese poetics .... It is clear that there is no true equivalent of metaphor in Chinese poetics." (Yeh, p. 252) Like his use of tragic structures, Kim's use of metaphor in "The Wedding Shoes" is western rather than Asian, as he focuses on poetic effect rather than on creating a harmonious view of the world.

Kim's attraction to Korean subjects and tragic effects is apparent in most of his other stories as well. One of his later stories, "Love in Winter," illustrates these interests as well as the problems Kim felt acutely in writing in a foreign language: "The language problem I was attacking loomed larger and larger as I began to learn more. When I would describe in English certain concepts and objects enmeshed in Korean emotion and imagination, I became slowly aware of nuances, of differences between two languages even in simple expression." (*Writer*, p. 28)   Kim often retained the Korean quality in his stories, so his writing is uniquely Korean. "Love in Winter" is another story filled with Korean nuances and motifs.   It is about a man with a physical deformity: a harelip. Mongche, the main character, hides this deformity behind a winter muff which he wears daily.   The Korean aspect to this tale is pronounced, for it is still not unusual in Korea to see men wearing muffs inside stores and on the streets.   Mongche falls in love with a girl who works in a small coffee shop, but he is afraid that if he shows his harelip to this girl he will be rejected. Enticed into helping in a robbery to raise money to have an operation to correct his harelip, he dies during the robbery.

Mongche is similar to Sangdo in many ways.   Both are young and   have fallen in love for the first time; both encounter a problem which leads to distress and acute unhappiness.   Sangdo is obsessed with his rejection;   his tragedy lies in the fact that he is not strong enough to try again.   Mongche is preoccupied with his physical deformity.   He is so convinced he will be rejected once his harelip is discovered he   doesn't give his girl a chance.   However, Sangdo loves or wants something that is outside himself, whereas Mongche has an psychological problem with his invalidity.   The common denominator is their hypersensitivity, which chains them to their unhappiness.   Both have tortured souls.   For example, Sangdo goes again and again to see the brocade shoes that constantly remind him of his emotional pain, while Mongche is unable to pull his scarf down when he speaks to Zee Ann, the girl he loves, and sips his cold tea when no one is looking. The men resolve their problems in different ways.   Sangdo seems to be able to overcome his difficulty, as   the war helps him to forget his past and pain.   Mongche on the other hand never seems to resolve his problem because it pertains to his inner soul.   The reason for Mongche's death lies precisely in his inability to cope with his spiritual difficulties.   His deformity becomes an obsession which is constantly rekindled by his father's cutting remarks.   At the beginning of the story, when Mongche laughs at a snowman, his father says sharply, "Don't go around the village opening your mouth like that.   I have told you ten thousand times whenever you laugh to hide your mouth with your hand. No one wants to see a harelip break into a smile." ("Love in Winter," p. 145) Thus, always conscious of his ugliness, Mongche hides behind his muff.

As in his other stories, Kim uses distinctly Korean images. His father's words, "He pains me like a fish bone in my throat," are a distinctly Korean expression. This simile is also appropriate because the story takes place in a fishing village. Elsewhere, "your belt is like the 38th parallel" refers to Korean geography. The title "Love in Winter" is used both realistically and metaphorically. The last line, "She would have been so lovely in spring" ("Love in Winter," p. 72), indicates that "winter" to Mongche is not only a season but also a state of mind. Korean stories during the Korean War are traditionally melancholy, so this reference is typically Korean.

The reader of "The Wedding Shoes" and "Love in Winter" is left with a feeling of sadness. This response is the intended one, for Kim's better stories are both very personal and very honest. As Kim once told me, "a writer must not be afraid to reveal himself." By telling the truth about life and himself Kim manages to communicate universal qualities to readers in very different cultures. Thus his "Wedding Shoes" was made into a European ballet, his stories have been translated into German, and two of his short stories became bestselling movies in Korea. Kim has made his Korean world and especially the village where he grew up come alive for a western audience.

Of the five writers in this study, Kim is the most Asian writer. However, it is interesting to note that he considers his pieces "drama[s] of human emotion." As Kim recalls, "One Saturday it was snowing really hard outside. I was filled with self-doubt and wondered how in the world I had acquired the fantastic idea that as a Korean I could write the drama of human emotion in fiction in a second language—no, in my third." (*Writer*, p. 29) The word "human" implies that although Kim's fictional world is limited, his aspiration has always been high. His first successful response came from Margette Young of Iowa Writer's Workshop. At her suggestion, he mailed a copy of "The Wedding Shoes" to Alice Morris, literary editor of *Harper's Bazaar*. (*Writer*, p. 30) Kim owes his first success to these two readers who appreciated his work. These two literary experts were able to see beyond the limitations of subject matter and locale. They judged the work according to its own principles. As Wayne Booth states, "Most of us can accept the essential poetic truth first formulated by Aristotle—that each successful imaginative work has its own life, its own soul, its own principles of being, quite independently of the prejudices or practical needs of this or that audience, and that our poetic devices should be an 'integral part of the whole.'" (Booth, p. 93) The life in Kim's stories is not only Korean but an artistic vision held together by many sophisticated literary devices.

Like other first generation Asian American writers, Kim relies on technique to overcome the language barriers not faced by second generation writers whose native language is English. Writing in a third language has been a difficult task for Kim, but he turns this liability into an asset. His Korean phrases do not sound like the broken English spoken by Lee's characters. Kim's expressions are Korean phrases translated word for word into English. The Korean American first generation reader can understand the value of these phrases better than the non-Korean American reader. However, for both readers the essence of the phrases does come across, adding an authentic flavor to the stories.

Due to its foreign setting and phrases, however, Kim's work is not widely appreciated by the general American audience. But of course it is as difficult to please all audiences as it is difficult to please everyone. Kim started writing about his own village because that is what he knew best. This has been sufficient to give him a special place as a short story writer in the Asian American literary world.

Chapter Four

Richard Kim:
Korean American Existentialist

In the study of Asian-American writers it is interesting to note that Richard Kim holds a unique place as an existentialist. Kim dedicated his first novel *The Martyred* to Albert Camus, "whose insight into 'a strange form of love' overcame for me the nihilism of the trenches and bunkers of Korea." In *The Martyred* the two main characters, Captain Lee and Mr. Shin, struggle to overcome precisely the enigma of nihilism. After a brief introduction to Richard Kim's personal background this chapter will focus on the existential theme and literary structure of *The Martyred* (1964) and *Lost Names* (1970), a third novel which is based on the first thirteen years of Kim's life. Percy Lubbock once remarked in reference to one of Henry James's contemporaries, "the author of the book was a craftsman, the critic must overtake him at his work and see how the book was made." (Lubbock, p. 274) To attempt to overtake Kim at his craft is an interesting and challenging task. Why is *The Martyred* considered an existential novel? How is it structured? What is its point of view? How is *Lost Names* different from *The Martyred* in its structure, viewpoint, and style? These are the questions this chapter attempts to answer.

Richard Kim, a Korean-American writer, was born in 1932 about ten years after Kim Yong Ik. His Korean name is Kim Eun Kook. Although "Kim" is a very common last name in Korea, Richard Kim and Kim Yong Ik are not related. Rather interestingly, Kim Yong Ik has kept his name in English in the same order as his Korean name. Richard Kim, however, has taken an American first name. Although both write for an American audience, Kim Yong Ik's style is distinctly Korean

while Richard Kim's is more western in nature. While Kim
Yong Ik's stories are primarily about personal relationships,
Richard Kim's novel *The Martyred* is about philosophical issues.
Kim Yong Ik's subject matter has been painful emotions;
Richard Kim's has been painful thoughts.

After World War II the existentialism of Sartre and Camus
perplexed and penetrated the thoughts of people all over the
world. *A Handbook to Literature* defines existentialism as "a
term applied to a group of attitudes current in philosophical,
religious, and artistic thought during and after the Second
World War, which emphasizes existence rather than essence
and sees the inadequacy of human reason to explain the
enigma of the universe as the basic philosophical question."
(Holman, pp. 192-193) For the existentialist, "Human beings
are totally free but they are also wholly responsible for what
they make of themselves. This freedom and responsibility are
the sources for their most intense anxiety." (Holman, p. 193)
This anxiety, inadequacy, and oppression permeated Kim's
own world as he grew up in one of the worst times in Korean
history. Despondency and desperation attacked the Korean
people daily. Korea was occupied by Japan until the end of
World War II. Shortly after the end of World War II Korea
found itself in another war, for North Korea attacked South
Korea in 1950 and the Korean War eventually lasted three
years. At the age of eighteen Richard Kim joined the South
Korean forces and wound up a liaison officer to the UN forces,
assigned to an English-speaking unit. (*Life*, p. 125) Looking
back at that period in his life, Richard Kim states in a preface
to *Korean Fantasia*, a book of Korean photographs organized by
a friend, John Chang McCurdy, "I am several years older than
John, but we together belong to that generation of Koreans
who had lived through and somehow survived the savage
brutalities and bloody, wanton destruction rained down by the
Korean War—that time in our lives when one suddenly
understood and shared the sort of mad, wrenching despair of
Shakespeare's King Lear—- 'As flies to wanton boys, are we to
the gods: They kill us for their sport.' But we had beaten
them at their own game." (McCurdy foreword, n. p.)

After the war ended in 1953, Kim came to the United States to study. First he majored in chemistry, which he failed. After changing his major to writing, he studied at the University of Iowa and attended Paul Engle's writing program where Kim Yong Ik had also studied. There he wrote *The Martyred*. Subsequently he received a Master's degree in Far Eastern literature at Harvard and has taught writing at the University of Massachusetts as an Adjunct Associate Professor since 1969.

Altogether Kim has written three books. *The Martyred* seems to have become a bestseller because readers after World War II were asking the same questions that the book posed. Written for English-speaking readers all over the world, the novel received excellent reviews. As Stephen Wilbers remarks, Kim's novel was reviewed on the front page of the *New York Times Book Review* by Chad Walsh, who called it "a magnificient achievement," and articles on the novel quickly appeared in *Life* and *Time* magazines. (Wilbers, p. 105) Pearl Buck called it 'an extraordinary book': "To take one incident and through it express the universal need of the human heart for God ... the agony of doubt combined with the longing to believe, is difficult indeed. Mr. Kim has accomplished just this .... A major achievement, in my opinion." (Kim, introduction to *The Martyred*, p. 5) Kim's second novel, *The Innocents* (1968), will not be discussed as it is not as well known or as significant as his first and third books. Kim's third book, *Lost Names*, which will be discussed first, is a more important work that is particularly interesting because it is autobiographical, a first-hand account of the Japanese occupation.

Lost Names is about the first thirteen years in Kim's life, 1932-1945. During this time Korea was occupied by Japan. After 1905 Japan steadily gained more and more control of Korea. By 1937 there was complete "Japanization": "use of the Japanese language was made mandatory in schools and in public places, and Korean history was dropped from their curriculum. Koreans were virtually compelled to adopt Japanese names and were required to participate in Shinto rituals." (Hoefer, p. 54) At this time the Japanese government interfered in every aspect of Korean life. In fact the Japanese tried to wipe out all traces of Korean heritage and culture.

Lost Names is based on a true account of the day when all Koreans, already required to speak only Japanese and bow to the Japanese emperor, had to change their Korean names to Japanese names.

Like Thoreau, Kim opens several of his chapters with the beginning of a new season, giving the book as a whole a circular effect—one of harmonious balance and acceptance. In *Walden* Thoreau condenses the twenty-two months from 1845 to 1847 he spent at Walden pond. *Lost Names* starts in winter in 1933 and ends thirteen years later. Winter is an appropriate opening for a story filled with hardships, beatings, and tears: "Snow flurries were swirling and swishing around all over—over the shabby little town, the snow-covered railway station, the ice-capped mountain, the frozen river, the bridge." (*Lost Names*, p. 3) Kim is only one-year old at the beginning of the book. He is carried in his mother's arms en route to Manchuria where his parents received offers to teach. On the train they become targets of suspicion by the Japanese police for being Christians. The father is taken away by the police and the mother waits in the freezing snow not knowing if he will come back. Finally, with several bruises on his face, the father does return to his family. After a long train ride, they cross a frozen river on foot to reach Manchuria.

The second and third chapters move forward in time but retain an ominous tone. The second chapter opens with the family back in Korea and describes Kim's first day at school. Kim is asked to sing. Unwittingly he sings an Irish song, "Danny Boy," for which he is punished and beaten. His Korean teacher tries to help him and is also beaten. Kim's assignment, his rebellion, and his punishment—all are byproducts of the Japanese occupation. At the beginning of the third chapter it is the end of August, a happy time when the school is on vacation. "I am awake—I have been awake for some time, basking in the glorious sunshine that seeps through the pale hue curtains on the window in my room, letting it touch my bare feet and make them feel warm and toasty." (*Lost Names*, p. 58) Several paragraphs later Kim continues, "It is summer, towards the end of August, sadly enough, but the school is still on vacation for another week or

so. In the summer, my parents and we, the children, go out to
our apple orchard and live in the cottage my father built on a
small knoll in the middle of the orchard." (*Lost Names*, p.59)
This chapter shows the close family relationship extending to
the grandparents who live with the family as do many
extended families in Korea. But the chapter also introduces
the theme of world war. The school teacher shows a map of
the world to the class with all the newly annexed countries
occupied by Germany, Italy, and Japan in 1937. The chapter
ends on a fearful note for Kim, who looks at the increasing
number and brilliance of the stars and is suddenly afraid of
the night sky as the stars remind him of all the places on the
map occupied by the enemy.

The fourth chapter, "Lost Names," is the most dismal in the
book. "It is February, the gloomiest and the cruelest time of
the interminable winter in our northern region. The sun
seldom ventures out in the dark heaven, as if it, too, finds
repugnant the dreary sky, ever shrouded with impenetrable
dirty grayness that tenaciously, almost perversely, defies the
light and its warmth." (*Lost Names*, p. 87) In this chapter the
Koreans are pushed to their limits. The scene of the Koreans
going to the police station to change their names to Japanese
names is quite movingly portrayed. The young Japanese
teacher visits Kim's family and apologizes for "inflicting on
you this humiliation ... unthinkable for one Asian people to
another Asian people, especially we Asians who should have a
greater respect for our ancestors ...!" (*Lost Names*, p. 109) Kim's
father is philosophical. "'The whole world is going mad, sir,'
says my father quietly,' going back into another dark age.
Japan is no exception.'" (*Lost Names*, p. 109) The fact that the
visitor is Japanese indicates that Kim does not intend to show
all Japanese as bad. It is interesting, however, that the teacher
is classified as being young, which implies that he is perhaps
less guilty of racial injustices.

The trip to the station is very painful. The father and son
meet an old man. "His tremulous voice says to my father,
'How can the world be cruel to us? We are now ruined – all of
us! Ruined!'" Kim comments as he looks back at this scene.
"And- suddenly – I am repelled by the pitiful sight of the

driveling, groveling old man whose whining muttering is lost
in the bitter wind and swirling snow. Turning away from him,
I stride down the path made by footsteps." (*Lost Names*, p. 112)
For a Korean to be asked to change his name is a cruel insult.
The Koreans are very conscious of their family. Once a year
they visit all the tombs of their ancestors. And they always
remember each dead relative on the anniversary of his death
by a family gathering, a feast, and a ritual of bowing to the
picture of the dead relative. These two occasions known as
Chusok and Jaysa are the two most important customs in
Korean culture. To make the Koreans change their names is
truly the cruelest of insults.

The last chapter, "In the Making of History - Together,"
ends in August. It is unpleasantly hot. "The brilliant sizzling
sun will appear in the clear blue sky, and the air will be filled
with the pungent odors of the muddy earth, wet trees, shrubs,
flowers, and thatched roofs drying, rendering our town
steaming and shimmering in the white heat of the sun." (*Lost
Names*, p. 160) Kim is thirteen when he hears the Japanese
emperor admitting defeat on the radio. "I am standing up,
not knowing how to control myself, trying to tell my grandfather that the Emperor is saying that Japan is surrendering to
the Allied powers unconditionally, but my voice is breaking,
and I am simply throwing myself onto him, sobbing." (*Lost
Names*, p. 162) This chapter is full of fast-moving actions. The
Koreans start mobbing the Japanese families. Kim's family
decides to hide a Japanese couple in their house in order to
save their lives. The father is released from a brief prison stay.
The Japanese commander commits hara kiri. Without fighting the Japanese give up all their control. Like others, Kim is
happy with "Tears shining in his eyes." The circular seasonal
pattern is appropriate because this form helps communicate
Kim's theme, which seems to be based on Ecclesiastes: "There
is a time for everything, and a season for every activity under
heaven." (*Ecclesiastes* lll: 1-2) Although Kim writes of bitter
experiences, his overall theme is one of acceptance. This
attitude is not only Christian but also distinctively Korean.
The Koreans believe that life consists of the yin and the yang,

two opposing forces. In fact, in the middle of the Korean flag there is a circle containing the yin and the yang.

The main events which Kim chooses to tell are those in school where he is beaten several times for being unknowingly nationalistic, those at home with his family, the trip to the police station, and finally the liberation. The main focus of the narrative is on the daily injustices of the Japanese occupation as it affected him and his family. Unfortunately, Kim's descriptions of the Japanese officials are not exaggerations; they are photographic. The book as a whole seems to aim at a fairly strict verisimilitude or realism. The story is told through the eyes of an adult looking back at his early life. Thus the viewpoint is that of an adult reflecting on his childhood. The use of the present tense, however, preserves immediacy. For example, in the first chapter the mother tells Kim what happened in 1933, when he was a baby: "'... and the twilight, yes, the twilight,' says my mother." (*Lost Names*, p. 3) The effect of the mother speaking in the present tense makes it seem as if she were speaking directly to the reader. The use of the present tense in relating events and feelings strengthens the bond between narrator and reader. In the third chapter Kim writes, "It is Sunday, and I have grown to dislike Sundays. Usually, on any other day during the vacation, my mother would let me sleep as long as I want, but a Sunday is a Sunday, and we have to get up early to make sure that my parents and my sister get to our church." (*Lost Names*, p. 61) In such passages the reader shares the immediate thoughts of an eleven-year-old narrator.

The writing style in *Lost Names* is more descriptive than that of *The Martyred*, and the sentences are much longer. For example, the following sentence goes on for half a page as Kim repeats the word "song" several times in the same sentence. "The big boy in the corner—he has his thumb and forefinger in front of his face, ready to squeeze his nose and say oink ... I stare at the back wall and then the large map of Europe, and my gaze shifts to the brown, wooden ceiling and then back to the map, and I concentrate on the map as if I have been asked to recite the names of the many little countries in Europe, thinking I must sing, I must sing my

favorite song ... but I have so many favorite songs, and I think
about all the songs I know and can sing and have sung ... I
have sung with my friends in Manchuria, my familiar friends
in Manchuria, with whom, only a week before, I was playing
and singing, all those friends I have left behind in
Manchuria — Korean, Chinese, Canadian, American, English
friends ... and I remember all their faces and gestures and the
songs we sang together." (*Lost Names*, p. 35) Here we enter
into an eleven-year-old's mind, and see his desire to please his
new teacher; at the same time we understand his nostalgia for
his old friends. The passage above illustrates Kim's first day in
school. At this time Kim has not yet experienced the harsh
realities of the Japanese occupation and how it will affect his
life at school. Kim's life thus far in Manchuria has been
happy. This is in contrast to the bitter realities he will soon
face in his new environment.

Kim also writes pages and pages of dialogue. Thus we get a
very clear picture of the family members as if watching the
drama on television. The book's seven chapters seem like
seven self-contained dramas, each vividly painted. The story is
told in the first chapter by the mother many years later to her
grown son. The other chapters are told by the son looking
back at his childhood. From this viewpoint the family seems
almost a perfect blend of great strength and patience. The
narrator does not refer to any of the family's weaknesses.
There is a clear line between the "good" characters, the
Koreans, and the "bad" characters, the Japanese. Nonetheless,
the ending of the book is emotionally satisfying because the
long suffering family as well as all the other Koreans, are
finally liberated when the Japanese surrender. This reaction is
perhaps similar to the emotional effect produced in a World
War II movie when the Germans surrender. Kim's portrait of
the Koreans versus the Japanese is quite subjective and
perhaps limited. However, I think that Kim wanted his
readers to share the pain that he suffered and rejoice with him
at the end of the novel. Thus, the emotionally satisfying
conclusion is the result of Kim's craftsmanship.

While *Lost Names* is emotionally satisfying, *The Martyred* is
intellectually satisfying. The two books reflect Kim's skill in

recreating a world he has lived through, though *The Martyred* goes on to question its essence. In *Lost Names* Kim narrates what happened to him and his family. In *The Martyred* he offers an existential novel that some have interpreted as an allegory about the nature of life itself. Here Kim addresses themes less confined to his own people and epoch.

As mentioned before, Kim leaves no doubt about his intentions by dedicating *The Martyred* "To the memory of Albert Camus, whose insight into 'a strange form of love' overcame for me the nihilism of the trenches and bunkers of Korea." A quotation from Holderlin's *The Death of Empedocles* is also included at the beginning of the book: "And openly I pledged my heart to the grave and suffering land, and often in the consecrated night, I promised to love her faithfully until death, unafraid, with her heavy burden of fatality, and never to despise a single one of her enigmas. Thus did I join myself to her with a mortal cord." This quotation is appropriate because Kim's underlying theme concerns existing in a world of baffling enigmas.

A mortal cord is weak and transitory. What then is the essence of existing in such a transitory state if there is no god? *The Martyred* questions the fundamental values of human existence, through the agonizing dilemma faced by Mr. Shin, the surviving minister. His agony is based on the fact that he is the only person who knows the answer to a terrible question, an answer that concludes the moral fable Kim unravels step by step through Captain Lee's eyes. At the beginning of the novel there are baffling questions. Fourteen ministers were captured by the North Communists. Twelve were killed but two survived. Why? Captain Lee, a central intelligence officer, is ordered to find out the answer by his superior, Colonel Chang. Colonel Chang desires to use this incident for propaganda purposes and wants to declare the twelve as martyrs. Captain Lee needs to find out not only the truth but also the reasons why the men behaved as they did. A simple assignment eventually becomes a quest for the mysteries and meaning of life, as in *Moby-Dick* when the search for the white whale becomes a symbolic quest for the mysteries of the universe. The answer is found in a Korean version of the existentialist philosophy.

The story is told through Captain Lee's eyes, thus limiting the reader to his viewpoint. Henry James suggests the importance of this technical decision in *The House of Fiction*: "[A man] and his neighbors are watching the same show, but one seeing more where the other sees less, one seeing black where the other sees white." (Stevick, p. 58)   The man can only report what he sees, black or white.   Norman Friedman defines the role of such a witness-narrator: "the natural consequence of this narrative frame is that the witness has no more than ordinary access to the mental states of others; its distinguishing characteristic, then, is that the author has surrendered his omniscience altogether regarding all other characters involved, and has chosen to allow his witness to tell the reader only what he as an observer may legitimately discover .... he therefore views the story from what may be called the wandering periphery." (Friedman, p. 125)   Thus, the reader travels with Captain Lee as he tries to find the truth.   As with Marlow in *Lord Jim*, however, there are other devices that the author uses to establish the relative credibility of this particular point of view.   For example, Mr. Shin's letters to Captain Lee are factual reinforcements supporting the relative reliability of Captain Lee's viewpoint. The comparison of Captain Lee to Marlow is most appropriate because Captain Lee serves a similar function in Kim's novel.   The main interest in *Lord Jim* is what happens to Lord Jim and not what happens to Marlow;   Marlow serves as an important device by which the story is told.   Likewise, the interest in *The Martyred* is not on what happens to Captain Lee but on the answer to his quest. In order to accomplish this objective, Captain Lee is used mainly as a "reporter" who must seem as reliable as possible. In *The Rhetoric of Fiction* Wayne Booth states, "For lack of better terms, I have called a narrator reliable when he speaks for or acts in accordance with the norms of the work (which is to say, the implied author's norms), unreliable when he does not." (Booth, p. 158)   Captain Lee fits the crucial criterion that Booth proposes for a reliable narrator.

Captain Lee's background makes him a credible narrator-witness. Before the war he was an instructor in Human Civilization—an appropriate subject for someone who is concerned with the meaning of life. He is also described as an intelligent person. To be a central intelligence officer one has to be a very sharp and perceptive person. He is also portrayed as a person one can trust. Further, Captain Lee has strong convictions about wanting the truth. "Truth must be told for the sake of its simply being the truth." (*The Martyred*, p. 106) He is trusted not only by the reader but also by the other characters in the novel. Even Mr. Shin tells him secrets he hasn't revealed to anyone else. Captain Lee uses logic rather than emotions. Unlike his boss, Colonel Chang, he is not overpowering in the conversations but listens carefully and then clearly states his opinions. Techniques such as interior monologue or stream of consciousness are not used, for the narrator provides us with an objective view of what is going on around him without adding too much of how he feels and thinks.

Unlike a novel such as Faulkner's *Absalom, Absalom!*, for example, where there are numerous narrators explaining the events of the novel, *The Martyred* has only one objective narrator to serve Kim's purpose. In *Absalom, Absalom!* the reader has to pause and think on what authority he is learning the facts. Each of the narrators tells the Sutpen story differently depending on how he feels or what he knows. For example, Rosa Coldfield's story is colored by her frustrations and hatred for Thomas Sutpen, Mr. Compson is unreliable because he doesn't know all the facts, and Quentin needs to make the Sutpen story as heroic as possible. Each of the narrators is working out his or her obsessions. Stylistically, this is like a symphony with many different rhythms and movements. By contrast, *The Martyred* resembles a highly absorbing newspaper account.

The writing is deliberately journalistic in several respects. The sentences are simple and staightforward. This quality fits in with Sartre's definition of literature. As Sartre states, "Prose is, in essence, utilitarian. I would readily define the prose-writer as a man who makes use of words." (Sartre, p. 10)

According to David Caute in his Introduction to *What is Literature?*, "Sartre's definition also tends to obscure the essential distinction between prose art (the novel, drama) and journalism .... This suggests that his distinction between prose and poetry is masking a value-judgment: his personal preferences for language which is descriptive and unembellished, a language tailored to express with urgency the most immediate issues of that time." (Sartre, p. viii) Kim's language is tailored to express the same issues.

Kim's style shows Camus's influence as well as Sartre's. Like Camus's, Kim's titles often start with the definite article: *The Rebel, The Stranger, The Plague; The Martyred, The Innocent.* I believe that Kim imitated Camus's style quite closely, and this use of the definite article is only one of many similarities. Others involve setting, characters' names, use of the sermon as a hortatory device, and the hint of resurrection at the end of the story. Camus and Kim are both quite self-conscious about style. Philip Thody quotes Camus as saying, "The truth is that I consider myself first and foremost an artist, and that problems of style and composition never cease to preoccupy me, especially when I refuse to cut myself off from the questions of the day." (Thody, p. 10) Kim might well have said the same thing.

Like Camus's, Kim's style is deliberately straightforward. Perhaps this is a quality that existential writers share, for Sartre also says in *What is Literature?*, "The function of a writer is to call a spade a spade .... There is nothing more deplorable than the literary practice which, I believe, is called poetic prose and which consists of using words for the obscure harmonics which resound about them and which are made up of vague meanings which are in contradiction with the clear meaning." (Sartre, p. 210) Kim agrees, for his own style is simple and understated. As Philip Roth has observed, "Mr. Kim's style allows for no adornment. It is written in a mood of total austerity, yet the passion of the book is perpetually beating up against its seemingly barren surface. Kim is concerned with the problems of the human condition and is a unique voice in any English-language fiction in his combination of modest style and grand theme." (Haslam, p. 109) Such observations are accurate. Whether the style exists for its own sake is another question, however. Booth comments perceptively on Sartre's writing method: "The existentialist novels, in contrast, will be 'toboggans, forgotten, unnoticed,' hurling the reader 'into the midst of a universe where there are no witnesses.' Novels should 'exist in the manner of things, of plants, of events, and not at first like products of man.' If this is so, the author must never summarize, never curtail a conversation, never telescope the events of three days into a paragraph." (Booth, p. 19) Booth further points out, "But as Sartre woefully admits .... even with all the forms of the author's voice expunged, what we have left will reveal to us a shameful artificiality." (Booth, p. 20) Booth concludes, "In short, the author's judgment is always present, always evident to anyone who knows how to look for it .... As we begin not to deal with this question, we must never forget though the author can to some extent choose his disguises, he can never choose to disappear." (Booth, p. 20)

I agree with Booth because the art of writing involves the arrangement of a work's elements for a purpose and an effect. A novel cannot exist like a plant; it cannot grow by itself. The second statement, that a novel exists like an event, is still harder to comprehend. How can a novel just exist or happen like an event? A work of art is not a living organism that develops by itself. Although Sartre's explanation sounds illuminating, upon close examination the passage turns out to be illogical. Kim's objective narration, his use of point of view, and his descriptive techniques are all part of a purpose that he has firmly envisioned. Thus, although Sartre, Camus, and Kim as existential writers advocate a simple style, their premises are different. While Sartre downplays the artistry of his works, Camus and Kim state clearly that they are artists. I think that Kim wanted to be considered an existential artist, and so he followed Camus closely.

There are especially interesting similarities between the description of the settings in *The Plague* and *The Martyred*. Consider this passage from Camus's novel:

The town, itself, let us admit, is ugly. It has a smug, placid air and you
need time to discover what it is that makes it different from so many
businesses of the world. How to conjure up a picture, for instance, of a
town without pigeons, without any trees or gardens, where you never
hear the beat of any winds or the rustle of leaves—a thoroughly negative place in short? (*The Plague*, p. 3)

Kim's description of the city of Pyongyang is as follows:

From the white-blue November sky of North Korea a cold gust swept
down the debris-ridden slope, whipping up here and there dazzling
snow flurries, smashing against the ugly, bullet-riddled building of
Pyongyang. People who had been digging in the ruins of their homes
stopped working. They straightened up and looked toward the top of
the slope, at the remains of the nearly demolished Central Church, and
then at the gray carcass of a cross-topped bell tower where the bell was
clanging. (*The Martyred*, p. 3)

The ugliness of the two cities and the prevailing mood of the
two passages are quite similar. In the first passage the description of a town without birds or plants and in the second
passage the words "carcass" and "remains" paint effectively the
picture of death. Like Oran, Pyongyang is a place
condemned. Instead of hundreds of rats in *The Plague*,
Pyongyang has hundreds of corpses piled all over the city.
Strong active verbs such as "swept down," "scooping up,"
"smashing against" and adjectives such as "debris ridden" and
"demolished" help create a vivid picture of a city in ruins.
Both paragraphs convey forcefully the dominant image of
destruction. The characters in these two novels are also
similar. In *The Plague* there is a doctor, a journalist, a crimi-
nal, a priest, and a legal official. In *The Martyred* there is an
army officer, his commanding officer, two ministers and a
chaplain. This makes the characters seem impersonal and
adds to the objective, even cold tone of each novel. As Thody
points out, "The constant understatement in the descriptive
style of *La Peste*, the precise use of administrative terms and
offical langauge, the deliberate banality of the words, are
essential elements in the final effect which the chronicle
makes. The impersonal mode of narration allows the author
to act on the reader's sensitivity without revealing his own, to
create emotion in the reader's mind by forcing him to project

his own feelings on to the extraordinary events so calmly described." (Thody, p. 109) Thody's remarks could be adapted very easily to *The Martyred*.

In *The Martyred* there are forty short chapters which progress like a journal. Many chapters indicate in the first paragraph what time of day it is. Chapter one starts, "The War came early one morning in June of 1950 ..." (*The Martyred*, p. 1) The next chapter begins after supper the next day, chapter eleven starts at midnight, chapter twelve starts the next morning, etc. This insistence on precise time is important because it helps create the impression that the story really happened. The story is set in a gray, concrete, and barren city as Kim offers a realistic portrayal of a city after a war. The pile of bodies is all too realistic and thematically appropriate. The narrator's voice attempts to infuse order into disorder. Captain Lee's voice remains stark and describes the surroundings in a flat, bleak tone. A major tenet of existentialism states that because God does not exist and cannot look out over the evil being of man, man must assume responsibility for his own actions. This makes life all the more frightening, especially when man's reason seems to have gotten out of hand. So the narrator's voice provides no solace but forces us to see the bleakness and horror of the city. Kim uses the state of the environment to help the reader understand what the narrator is thinking or feeling. The fact that the narrator makes frequent references to the cold and dark weather reinforces the general tone of the novel. The main settings are Colonel Chang's office, the church, and Mr. Shin's house. All of these settings mirror the dismal effects of war. Thus the use of objective correlatives is quite effective in building up the desolate tone.

All of the techniques mentioned above are devices that Kim uses to help unlock the moral essence of his novel. Captain Lee's search leads him to find Mr. Hann, who has become insane, and Mr. Shin, who still practices Christianity. Captain Lee witnesses Mr. Shin's confessions before his congregation: "I was a sinner. I was a weakling. I was defeated. Blessed by the names of your martyreds! For they forgave me. And they died in the name of our Lord." (*The Martyred*, p. 159) This confession infuriates the congregation, and they denounce Mr. Shin as a traitor. The narrative poses the question of whether we should respond in the same fashion.

Captain Lee wants to know why Mr. Shin is lying because earlier he heard the captured North Korean officer, Major Jung, admit: "It gives me great pleasure to tell you that your great heroes and martyrs died like dogs. Like dogs, whimpering, whining, wailing. It pleased me to hear them beg for mercy, to hear them denounce their god and one another. They died like dogs. Like dogs, do you hear?" (*The Martyred*, p. 97) When asked why Mr. Shin was not killed, Major Jung replies, "He was the only one who put up a fight. I like a good fight. He had guts. He was the only one who had enough guts to spit in my face." (*The Martyred*, p. 98) Thus, Captain Lee confronts Mr. Shin: "'Mr. Shin, Mr. Shin! Why all that!' I said in desperation. 'Why all that, why deceive your people, when our sufferings here and now have no justice to seek for beyond this life?'" "'All my life I have searched for God, Captain,' he whispered,' but I found only man with all his sufferings .... and death, inexorable death!'" "And after death?" "'Nothing,' he whispered. 'Nothing!'" (*The Martyred*, p. 184) Mr. Shin admits that he lies to his people to give them "the illusion of hope": "Despair is the disease of those weary of life, life here and now full of meaningless sufferings. We must fight despair, we must destroy it and not let the sickness of despair corrupt the life of man and reduce him to a mere scarescrow." Captain Lee asks: "And you? What about you? What about your despair?" "That is my cross!" Mr. Shin responds. "I must bear that alone." (*The Martyred*, p. 185)

Most Christian ministers are able to bear any burden and sacrifice if strengthened by the assurance that they will be rewarded in heaven. In Mr. Shin's case he acts without such assurance. He wants his congregation to believe that the twelve ministers died as true martyrs for a God in whom he himself does not believe.

Why does Mr. Shin lie? He tells Captain Lee that he does so to give his congregation hope. In other words, he is using and not serving God. He is a false minister, one who preaches Christianity but does not believe that God exists. Can it be that he is doing what he does because he is from a group-oriented society? The Korean culture is definitely group-oriented. Traditionally, it has not been unusual for a person to sacrifice himself for his family, friends, or country. The samurais in ancient Japan and the kamikaze pilots in World War II killed themselves for the honor of their families or country. In Mr. Shin's case his sacrifice is for his congregation. Mr. Shin's fate is ambiguous and left open at the end of the book. Chaplain Koh states, "If I were to believe all of their stories, well, Mr. Shin is everywhere in North Korea. Some thought that he was executed and some thought that he had seen him living somewhere." (*The Martyred*, p. 225) Mr. Shin seems to have been resurrected like Christ and seen at different places by different people. Thus the author clearly wants to make Mr. Shin a Christ figure.

Despite their divergent beliefs, both Mr. Shin and Captain Lee understand the anxiety and enigma of life without a God. This awareness brings them together and makes them both heroes. Mr. Shin's actions make him an ironic Christ figure. He does not believe in God, but he preaches and seems to love others more than himself. He uses the gospel to give the people hope despite the fact that the congregation treats him as a Judas. In short, he loves others when they hate him. This is his existential stand.

At the end of his search Captain Lee finds "a wondrous lightness of heart": "I walked away from the church, past the rows of tents where silent suffering gnawed at the hearts of people — my people — and headed toward the beach, which faced the open sea. There a group of refugees gathered under the starry dome of the night sky, were humming in unison a song of homage to their homeland. And with a wondrous lightness of heart hitherto unknown to me I joined them." (*The Martyred*, p. 228) That Captain Lee joins in the singing at the end concludes the novel on a very positive note. In the last paragraph of the novel a "lightness of heart hitherto unknown to me" moves Captain Lee to join in the singing just as Tommy Wilhelm in Saul Bellow's *Seize the Day* is moved to overwhelming tears as he see the dead body of a stranger in a church. Whether Captain Lee would be a changed person if the novel were to continue is questionable. It seems to be a momentary uplifting that does not altogether break the the cold, even ice-like voice of the novel.

What then is the author's point of view? Would he use the ideas of existentialism and dedicate the book to Camus if he didn't have a similar point of view? Richard Kim is making a statement and taking a stand on existentialism even though his narrator doesn't seem to be doing so. The fact that the book is arranged in a particular way, the fact that clues appear in every chapter to keep the reader interested and at the same time thinking about the question of existence, and the fact that Mr. Shin makes his existential stand point to the conclusion that Kim had a definite theme in mind. As R. S. Crane states in "The Concept of Plot and the Plot of *Tom Jones*," "It follows ... that the plot, considered formally, of any imitative work is, in relation to the work as a whole, not simply a means—a 'framework' or 'mere mechanism'—but rather the final end which everything in the work, if that is to be felt as a whole, must be made, directly or indirectly to serve." (Friedman, p. 144) The plot in this case does embody the novel's theme. The quest around which the plot evolves finds its answer in the theme. Mr. Shin behaves the way he does because he believes in a kind of existentialism. Kim's fable is that the true martyr is one who lives for others. Man must exist for humanity and not God. For Kim, what one does for others is what really counts.

The title *The Martyred* is itself allegorical. However, the definition of a martyr is not rooted in Christianity, but in an unusual form of existentialism. In the following sermon Mr. Shin confesses to his congregation: "He told the hushed congregation how the martyrs resisted their captors ... The ministers were offered, in turn, a promise that a post in the government cabinet would be given to a representative of the Christians, that those Christians held by the Communists as political prisoners would be freed unconditionally, and the property of the churches would not be confiscated by the regime. They refused everything, and they were tortured... But your martyrs were not defeated; they defied the torturers. But my brethren, I could not. I did not!" (*The Martyred*, p. 140)

Mr. Shin goes on to explain how the martyrs died and he survived because he gave in. At the end of the sermon, he urges the congregation, "You! Sinners! Down, down on your knees and repent! I say unto you into the name of your martyrs, repent, ye sinners, for my sins and for your sins. Repent!" (*The Martyred*, p. 141) The irony of this sermon lies in the fact that everything Mr. Shin has just said is untrue. In fact the reverse is true. Mr. Shin is the only person who survived because he was the only person who was strong enough to stand up to his captors. The horrible truth is that Mr. Shin does not believe in god.

As Paneloux and Rieux debate the nature of God in *The Plague*, Captain Lee and Mr. Shin have a similar debate. The purpose of the debate is to clarify the two characters' viewpoints. When Captain Lee asks Mr. Shin why he has lied to his congregation, Mr. Shin replies, "Because they are men. Despair is the disease of those weary of life, life here and now full of meaningless sufferings. We must fight despair, we must destroy it and not let the sickness of despair corrupt the life of man and reduce him to a mere scarecrow." (*The Martyred*, p. 185) This statement unlocks the novel's theme. According to Kim there is no God. Mr. Shin does not believe in God but he lies to give his people hope. This knowledge is his "cross." Kim has cast Mr. Shin as the real martyr. Thus, Richard Kim has created a cast of Korean characters in a Korean setting to explore a moral question of universal appeal. In *The Martyred* existentialism has been transformed into a memorable Korean model of the philosophy's essence.

The Martyred is Kim's most successful book due to its appeal to a large audience. *Lost Names* has not achieved similar recognition because of its limited scope and subject matter. Although both stories take place during important historical periods in Korean history, the Korean War and the Japanese occupation during World War II, we have seen that the two books are very different in style and subject matter. The Korean-American audience finds *Lost Names* particularly interesting. For first generation Korean Americans, the book depicts their own painful memories. For second generation Korean Americans, the book helps them understand their heritage. Both Korean-American audiences sympathize with Kim's patriotic book about Koreans. It is more difficult for a non-Korean American audience to truly understand the Korean experience. Thus, the non-Korean American audience has preferred *The Martyred*, the one novel by Richard Kim in which he goes well beyond the limitations of his Korean heritage.

Chapter Five

Yoshiko Uchida's Positive Vision

Yoshiko Uchida is a second generation Japanese American writer who grew up in California in the 1940's. According to the *San Francisco Examiner*, "Her father, Dwight Takashi Uchida, worked as a 'salaried man' at the San Francisco branch of Mitusi and Co., one of Japan's foremost trading firms. Her mother, Iku, was an accomplished poet and often composed tanka, or verses, for her family." (*San Francisco Examiner*, p. S-6) Uchida graduated from the University of California cum laude. According to Thomas James, a social historian, "Yoshiko Uchida, one of these Nisei teachers, had just finished her undergraduate studies at the University of California when her family was evacuated from Berkeley. She received her diploma in the mail while living in a horse stall that had been converted into living quarters at the Tanforan race track, which was serving as an assembly center until more permanent facilities could be constructed in the interior of the country." (James, p. 28) After the war she continued her education at Smith College, where she received a Master's degree in Education, and then turned to teaching and writing.

Uchida is primarily a children's author although her most recent book, *Picture Bride* (1987), is written for adults. Her books have won numerous awards and been recognized by the Junior Literary Guild, the American Library Association, and the Commonwealth Club of America. Very little research has been done on her works, however, as the general neglect of Asian American literature is even more pronounced when the author is writing for children.

Uchida's books tell much the same story in many different ways. This story is about a Japanese girl growing up during World War II in America. Indeed, it was a hard time for a

Japanese American to be living in America. As James notes, "Representative John E. Rankin of Mississippi ... agreed with his colleagues from California on the necessity of evacuation. 'Once a Jap, always a Jap. We cannot afford to trust any of them.'" (James, p. 23) Statements like these were all too frequent. Eventually they led to legislation and internment of the Japanese in relocation camps.

The story that is retold and repeated in Uchida's books has a constant cast of characters drawn from her own family. As Annie Nakao states, "like patches on a family quilt, the characters of children's book author Yoshiko Uchida are composites of her own child's eye view of Berkeley in the 1930's." (*San Francisco Examiner* p. S-2) The same characters reappear in each story: the father, the mother, a twelve-year-old girl, a brother or brothers. "Her stories ... evoke a sense of family that was so strong among the Issei. They had a sense of purpose, a strength of support that is so important for people to remember." (*San Francisco Examiner*, p. S-6) The "issei" are first generation Japanese who tend to be quite traditional in their conduct. In each of the stories the parents, in particular the mother, display great strength when faced with discrimination or adversity. Not only the characterizations but the plots and themes of the four books are related. They do, indeed, fit a pattern in which the family undergoes trials both spiritual and physical but eventually manages to persist. One sees this pattern in the four books to be discussed. Although Uchida has written about twenty-five books including folktales, poetry, and adult non-fiction, I have chosen four books because they are about the Asian American experience: *Journey to Topaz* (1971), *Journey Home* (1978), *A Jar of Dreams* (1981), and *Picture Bride* (1987).

The other three books to be discussed seem like sequels to *Journey to Topaz*. This book is about the Sakane family during their stay at a relocation camp at Topaz. In her prologue Uchida provides perspective on the situation: "On February 19, 1942, President D. Roosevelt issued an executive order which authorized the Secretary of War 'to prescribe areas from which any or all persons may be excluded '.... This order cleared the indiscriminate removal of 110,000 persons of

Japanese ancestry, without hearings of any kind, from the entire West Coast. All Japanese were uprooted from their homes and sent to inland camps to be held behind barbed wire. Two-thirds of these people were American citizens and I was one of them .... *Journey to Topaz* is the story of one Japanese family and what happened to them as a result of the evacuation orders. Although the characters are fictitious, the events are based on actual fact, and much that happened to the Sakane family also happened to my own." (*Journey to Topaz*, pp. vii-viii) The Uchidas entered one of sixteen temporary assembly centers in the Pacific Coast sometime between March and June of 1942. (James, p. 29)

Yuki's family consists of her father, her mother, and an older eighteen-year-old brother, Ken. Because the story is written for the eight to twelve-year-old audience, the tone is light and positive despite the circumstances. A limited third-person point of view is used. The author reports how Yuki sees the reactions of her family to their situation. The author explains the feelings and thoughts of Yuki, who thinks according to her age and background. The hard reality of the suffering of the imprisoned Japanese Americans is not emphasized. The book certainly does not have an angry tone; rather it treats hardship much as Esther does in Dickens' *Bleak House* or the March family in Alcott's *Little Women*.

The American reader is introduced to the fundamental values of a Japanese American family. "Everyone acknowledged the fact that Father was head of the house and everyone listened with respect when he spoke. He had been in America four years longer than Mother, but he was proud of her heritage. He was the grandson of a samurai and he behaved like one. He was brave and dignified and behind his strength was a gentle heart." (*Journey to Topaz*, p. 17) Warriors and noblemen in ancient Japan, the samurai lived by a strong sense of honor and code of conduct. All Yuki knows about a samurai is what she has been told, but she is taught to respect and follow the family code of conduct. At the beginning of the book, when the FBI takes the father away simply because he is one of the leaders of the Japanese American community, the eighteen-year-old son, Ken, and not the mother replaces the father as head of the house. "More and more Ken was taking over as head of the house. Father signed the car over to him so it could be sold, and Ken was able to withdraw money from Father's account." (*Journey to Topaz*, p. 35) The mother also behaves as a traditional Japanese wife who is always subservient to her husband. For example, "she still sat in the back seat of the car instead of in front beside Father. She was a gentle Japanese lady, but she also had a strong and noble spirit." (*Journey to Topaz*, p. 18) Thus, the family lives according to traditional Japanese values.

Within the general framework of the plot, two main questions keep the story interesting. The two questions are: what has happened to Father, and why does Ken change? Father returns in chapter fifteen, and Ken changes due to his increasing bitterness about the way the Japanese are treated. Ken decides to join the all-volunteer Japanese American army in Europe rather than go to college. Other significant events include the tragic killing of an old neighbor, Mr. Kurihara. Mr. Kurihara is killed while trying to look for new plants near the fence because the military thinks he is trying to escape. This episode mirrors reality, for, according to James, "In the relocation centers, the military controlled ... the fence and gate, regulating all entry and exit, day and night, after the fences were built in 1942." (James, p. 33) Another tragic event is a friend's struggle with tuberculosis. In addition, the Japanese who feel that Yuki's family is too cooperative with the American authorities throw a bomb at their shelter. Uchida's story therefore mirrors the unpleasant realities of the period.

Despite the tragic events, there are moments of kindness that shine out. The family has American friends who visit them at the camp with delicious food. There is also the wonderful dinner to which Yuki's family is invited before their trip to the camp. This is to remind the reader that not all Americans disliked the Japanese. The Japanese also care for each other within the camp. The mother's attitude is always positive. She even gives tea and refreshment to the FBI men who come to inspect their home. Such actions counteract the discrimination and pain depicted in the story. The author does not dramatize events to evoke pity or anger. Instead she reveals the circumstances through the innocent eyes of a child. This perspective draws a child's emotional response from the adult reader. A critic once said that great literature must first aim at the heart. If we apply this dictum to children's literature, then Yoshida's use of a simple child's voice is perhaps the best way to get directly at certain basic emotions. It seems that in this case a simple child's voice works more effectively than all the rhetorical devices or other points of view Uchida might have used.

The mother in this book is very much like Mrs. March in *Little Women* who goes to help the poor despite her own needy situation. Seen through the eyes of an eleven-year-old daughter there seems to be no weakness in her. The mother in Uchida's story is very careful to obey the law. "Mother was anxious to observe every letter of the law. As soon as it was required that enemy aliens register, she had gone immediately to get registered." (*Journey to Topaz*, p. 32) Her strength goes beyond such realistic conformity, however, and since Father does not reappear until the last two chapters of the book, the mother is the dominant force in the family. On the day before they leave for the camp the mother cleans the house thoroughly. "But Mother was neat and conscientious to the very end. 'Of course it matters,' she said, "I want to leave a nice clean house for whoever will rent it after we're gone." (*Journey to Topaz*, pp. 41-42) Even at the camp the mother makes sure that everything is clean and attractive and also sends for seeds to plant. "Mother had sent out for some flower seeds and planted them in a small patch of ground in front of their stall. The summer sun and the manure-rich soil had produced a beautiful crop of stocks, petunias, and zinnias that brightened the patch of earth around them. Mother said she would rather have flowers to look at than laundered clothes and she didn't have clothes lines put up in front of their stall as many of the people had done." (*Journey to Topaz*, p. 77) This passage indicates the mother's positive attitude about life. She does not submit to despair. Instead she thinks of ways to uplift her family's and her own spirit. This positive outlook on life is what Uchida wants to convey to her readers.

Food is mentioned several times in the novel to convey loving care. Mrs. Nelson, a kind neighbor, invites them to dinner the night before they are to leave for camp. "Mimi's mother invited them to dinner on their last night. She made roast turkey with all the trimmings, as though it were Thanksgiving or Christmas. And for dessert she baked two different kinds of pie so Ken could have a piece of each." (*Journey to Topaz*, p. 42) Upon arrival at the camp, Mr. Toda, a friend, brings them a bag of peanuts. "Yuki ate one peanut at a time, chewing carefully and slowly, savoring each small bit." (*Journey to Topaz*, p. 56) When Mrs. Nelson and Mrs. Jamieson visit them at the Tanforan camp they bring a chocolate cake and crackers, cheese and nuts and cookies. In contrast, the lack of good things to eat reinforces the underlying theme of misery. "You know what I'd like right now?" Ken asked. "A nice juicy steak, medium rare, with onions on the side and a big baked potato full of sour cream, and a huge piece of apple pie with cream and ..." "Stop it!" Yuki shrieked. "You're giving me hunger pangs." The mother replies, "I don't even have any candy." As Uchida comments, "It was a sad day for Mother when she couldn't offer something good to eat to provide her family some comfort." (*Journey to Topaz*, p. 55)

The passages above show how Uchida selects certain moments to reinforce the idea of hunger in a very natural way. The following passage also demonstrates this technique. When Ken decides to stay with Yuki and Mother rather than go to college, Yuki decides to give him a long saved chocolate bar. "Yuki simply had to do something nice for Ken. She went to her shelf and got out a chocolate bar from Mimi that she'd been saving for herself. She was tempted to break it in half and go halves with Ken, but in a burst of generosity, she gave him the whole bar." (*Journey to Topaz*, p. 82) When the father returns they celebrate with cookies and candy and fruit saved from the mess hall. "It seemed almost like the busy happy days back in Berkeley, and Mother served tea and crackers and Spam and cheese that she had found at the canteen." (*Journey to Topaz*, p. 127) Thus, food or the lack of food is a major plot device. It is also appropriate because the twelve-year-old reader can easily identify with and visualize the food scenes.

Uchida also uses the weather as a device to tie the story together thematically. The book starts in December on "a cold gloomy Sunday." In addition, "Today looked like snow weather for the sky was gray and murky, but only with fog that blew in cold and damp from San Francisco Bay." (*Journey to Topaz*, p. 1) The weather is described realistically and at the same time sets the tone for a book that does deal with "colder" realities than one usually associates with children's books. James tells us that "the dust storms at Topaz were so ferocious that all movement and conversation stopped for the interim, whether for minutes or hours." (*James*, p. 47) Topaz is described by Uchida as a place with "no vegetation at all and they were surrounded by a vast gray-white desert where nothing grew except dry clumps of greasewood." (*Journey to Topaz*, p. 94) This is a realistic description of a deserted area in Utah, but it also conveys   Uchida's feelings about the unattractive place and experience. Finally, at the end of the story when they return to Berkeley, "It was as though she was seeing the whole world with new eyes. The colors seemed brighter, the air seemed fresher, the sounds sharper. It was as though she had climbed out of a cocoon and suddenly discovered the sun." (*Journey to Topaz*, p. 149) The clear sky contrasts with the dusty skies of Topaz and thus marks a release from the camp. The book as a whole projects such affirmations even as it acknowledges unpleasant realities often excluded from such works.

Journey Home is a continuation of *Journey to Topaz*. *Journey Home* was a Junior Guild Selection as an outstanding book and seems to many people an advance on its predecessor. The structure of this book can be divided into eight parts: 1. the family's release from camp; 2. their life in Salt Lake City; 3. their return to Berkeley; 4. their grocery catching fire; 5. the forming of new friendships; 6. Ken's return from war; 7. Ken's lingering bitterness; 8. overcoming the effects of war. These sections combine to form an effective, moving action. The title is also effective because not only do the characters return to their home, Berkeley, but they also accept their new situation with renewed hopefulness.

The characters of this second novel reveal the same concerns as in the first book. The father and mother are again portrayed as positive and patient. The reader is again reminded that this is a proud Japanese family. "Yuki's grandfathers had died in Japan long before she was born. They had both been brave samurai warriors in years long past and that was something to be proud of. It meant Yuki and her brother were the grandchildren of two samurai, so they had to be brave and courageous and loyal too. It meant being strong when necessary, but still having a gentle heart capable of loving beautiful things. It meant they had a past to live up to, and Yuki wasn't sure she could manage." (*Journey Home*, p. 19) Yuki manages to overcome, however, with the help of her mother. Yuki is depicted as a sensitive adolescent who must cope with such problems as discrimination, as when she goes to the restroom on a bus. "Just as she opened the door to go in, a blond woman with two small children pushed past her. She glared angrily at Yuki and muttered, 'Go back where you belong, you damn Jap.'" (*Journey Home*, p. 43) Here as elsewhere, her mother's presence strengthens Yuki: "but Mama reminded her how much nicer this was than the long train ride going in the other direction." (*Journey Home*, p. 44) Like the Yuki of *Journey to Topaz*, Yuki gets accustomed to discrimination and doesn't let it overwhelm her.

Uchida also uses the element of the supernatural because the Japanese are often superstitious. Thus, the Sakane family, although they are Christians, attribute certain events to the unseen. Superstition also serves to foretell events that will follow in the story. When Yuki breaks her mother's cherished vase, the mother isn't upset. Instead, "Mama smiled a sort of half-smile, as though she were remembering something from long ago. 'That's what your grandma would have said, Yuki. She used to say that objects sometimes have lives of their own and that sometimes they die in order to spare us.'" (*Journey Home*, p. 31) When they receive a telegram from Ken, the family is relieved because they were so afraid that he had been killed. The mother says, "you know, good things often happen in threes. Maybe two more nice things will happen before long." (*Journey Home* p. 39) The family soon learns that the exclusion order against the Japanese on the West Coast has been revoked and they can return to Berkeley. The supernatural foretelling does not provide any conflict with their religious beliefs. As mentioned before, the family leads a devoted Christian life. Christmas occurs in chapter five of *Journey Home* and in chapter one of *Journey to Topaz*. The mother reminds Yuki, "Maybe the world has gone crazy ... but the Christmas story is still the same. It's important to remember that, Yuki, and not forget what Christmas really means." (*Journey Home*, p. 34) Her religion, then, is one of the ways in which Mama is definitely a strong positive influence for Yuki.

As the family starts to rebuild their lives, they encounter hardship as well as friendship. In this they are typical; as James states, "But as Japanese immigrants worked to make a place for themselves in American society, they were opposed by organized interests and influential newspapers." (James, p. 14) An eight o'clock curfew is set for all Japanese. The family is opposed by the general public, and their grocery store is even set on fire. Two strangers, however, come to help them rebuild. Mr. and Mrs. Olssen's own son was killed by the Japanese in World War II, but this couple volunteers to help a Japanese America family rebuild their demolished store. Thus Uchida points out that individuals can be kind despite official restrictions against the Japanese.

We can most clearly see this pattern of reconcilation in Ken's characterization. The return home is not only a physical one but a state of mind as well. Ken returns from the war with a broken leg and a shattered spirit. His brooding and sullen attitude bothers his family. Ken thinks constantly about the death of his best friend, Jim, and his own crippled leg. Grandfather Oka and Ken's father confront Ken and try to comfort him. "Ken, you're a survivor, just as we all are — your mama, Mr. Oka, Grandma Kurihara and I. We're survivors from another land — the land of your samurai grandfathers. Their strength was our strength as we struggled to make new lives for ourselves in America. Make it your strength too, Ken. Hold on to it and be strong." (*Journey Home*, p. 129) The message finally hits Ken. At the end of the book, he decides to give up his bitterness and go on living in a more positive way. Thus at the end Yuki concludes, "Everyone she cared about was here with her now. They'd all come home at last, even Ken. And Yuki knew that everything was going to be all right. She'd finally come home too." (*Journey Home*, p. 131) Thus all the family members recover from the effects of war. They are able to forgive and forget and look ahead with hope. As in *Journey to Topaz*, the moral fable of *Journey Home* is about the need to possess inner strength despite difficult circumstances.

Before examining *A Jar of Dreams* it is interesting to note the point of view in *Journey Home*. The story is told mainly from the third person limited omniscient point of view. In chapter one we enter the mind of Yuki with the use of the flashback dream. We are reminded that the story is a sequel to *Journey to Topaz* because Yuki dreams that she is encountering the dusty storms at Topaz. We see the other characters as Yuki sees them, for the viewpoint is Yuki's even though she is not the narrator. This makes for dramatic concentration and continuity because Uchida focuses on the mind of a single person. The story is what Yuki knows, not what Ken knows or what Mama knows. Among others, Jane Austen used this method in *Emma* and Henry James in *The Ambassadors*, with Austen producing especially effective dramatic irony by using this point of view. In *Journey Home*, however, irony is not intended. This is a more straightforward book, less interested in subtle psychological discriminations. This limited point of view is appropriate for the younger audience because the story is about what the audience itself can relate to. The twelve-year-old Yuki provides the right viewpoint character because her early adolescent audience can identify with her.

By contrast, *A Jar of Dreams* is told in the first person. The use of the first person in this book allows for greater intimacy and facilitates more direct reader identification. It also permits greater emotional impact. Phyllis Whitney, a well-known children's author, has said, "I find there is a sense of immediacy to the first person that lends itself to a building of suspense." (Whitney, p. 77) As Whitney further observes, "If you want your story to carry an emotional impact, it is wise to select one character and tell the story from his viewpoint from beginning to end." (Whitney, p. 75) This approach is even more effective in the first person. Here the language and words are those of Rinko, a twelve-year-old. Hers is a consistent voice with typical idiomatic expressions, much like Huck Finn's voice in *Huckleberry Finn*. For example, she describes her brother in her own vivid language: "Joji is growing sideways instead of up. And like me, he also missed out on the wavy hair and large eyes." (*A Jar of Dreams*, p. 15) Rinko thinks of herself as a "big nothing." Rinko, born in the United States, speaks English like an American. Her English is unlike her parents', and Uchida's use of her voice suggests that Uchida's audience is very much American rather than Japanese or even Japanese American. Uchida is writing for all Americans, as her message is for all humanity.

A Jar of Dreams is about the same family with different names. The cast of characters are Mama, Papa, Rinko, and two brothers, Jijo and Cal. As in previous stories, we have two kind American ladies. In addition there are the usual people who are anti-Japanese. We are introduced to one significant new character, Aunt Waka, from Japan. These characters have different dreams that tend to identify them here as in the earlier stories. In *Journey Home* Papa's dream is to open a grocery store and Ken's dream is to become a doctor. In *Picture Bride* Hana's hope is to attain a more secure economic status. Likewise in *A Jar of Dreams*, Papa's dream is to open a garage shop. "Papa says some day, when he's paid up all his debts, he's going to get rid of the barbershop and open up a garage and repair shop. That's only one of his dreams, and he's always telling us not to be afraid to have all the big dreams we want." (*A Jar of Dream*, pp. 7-8) Rinko dreams of becoming a school teacher, "even though my older brother, Cal, says no public school in California would ever hire a Japanese teacher." (*A Jar of Dreams*, p. 8) Before she married the mother's dream was to become a school teacher herself. "She squinted at the old photograph and began to smile. 'Do you know I wanted to become a school teacher then?' she asked. I was surprised. I'd never before imagined Mama wanting to be anything else than exactly what she was now. It never occurred to me she might have had another kind of dream for herself." (*A Jar of Dreams*, p. 36)   Despite their dreams, the father struggles with his barbershop that eventually fails and Cal studies engineering despite the fact that there is little hope of his succeeding.

Two events are key structural points in this novel about a family's various dreams.   The first is Aunt Waka's arrival, anticipated throughout the first forty-eight pages (five whole chapters).   The second is the episode involving Wilbur Starr. The Starr family tries to prevent the Tsujimuras from going into the home laundry business because they fear the competition.   There are several incidents which make up the rising action of the conflict.   First the Tsujimuras receive a note: "It was printed in large black letters and said, 'GET OUT OF OUR TERRITORY JAP LAUNDRY, OR YOU'LL BE SORRY.'" (*A Jar of Dreams*, pp. 61-62)   Next their bundles of laundry get stolen.   Papa and Uncle Kanda finally visit Wilbur Starr to confront him.   As Rinko narrates, "From that day on, everything on my mind was either B.W.S. (Before Wilbur Starr), or A.W.S. (After Wilbur Starr), sort of like B.C. and A. D. in history." (*A Jar of Dreams*, p. 94)

The confrontation finally occurs at the suggestion of Aunt Waka and Mrs. Sugar, who argue that they should stand up to the Starrs.   Papa and Uncle Kanda visit Wilbur Starr, who just glares at them and speaks with contempt: "You people are all alike, undercutting us with your cheap labor and cheap prices. That's bad for all of us.   Why don't you just go on back where you came from?" (*A Jar of Dreams*, p. 89)   Rinko observes that the father does not run but stands up to Wilbur Starr: "I looked at Wilbur Starr and saw his mouth was open, but no words were coming out.   His eyes bulged and he took off his eyeshade and wiped his forehead.   Until now he'd always thrown a lot of hateful words at us and watched us run.   But Papa hadn't run.   He and Uncle Kanda had told him exactly what they thought of him, and Wilbur Starr looked like he'd run clean out of words." (*A Jar of Dreams*, p. 91)   As they leave Rinko notices that "his mouth was hanging open like a sick dog's and he looked like he'd just swallowed a mouthful of hot chili and didn't know what to do with his face.   I knew I'd remember that look on his face as long as I lived. And I also knew than I'd never be afraid of him again. None of us would." (*A Jar of Dreams*, p. 92) This anticipates the resolution that Rinko reaches at the end of the story.

The story ends with Aunt Waka's departure. "I guess Aunt Waka had stirred us up and changed us all so we'd never be quite the same again. I was really beginning to feel better about myself—even the part of me that was Japanese—and I almost looked forward to going back to school to see if maybe things would be different." (*A Jar of Dreams*, p. 130) The word "maybe" gives the statement a sad touch. The reader knows that things probably will not change dramatically. However, Rinko is able to become a stronger person at the end of the book, a change mirrored in the rest of her family who resolve to pursue their dreams whether they are successful or not. Thematically this is quite appropriate for an audience of children or early adolescents. The novel deals with courage in the face of discrimination; it encourages readers to develop just such strength of character.

In examining the structure of the book, it is interesting to note that Uchida uses several devices to move the story forward effectively. For example, she tends to create an element of suspense at the end of each chapter. At the end of chapter one the last sentence states, "And it wasn't until after supper that I found out what it [Papa's problem] was." (*A Jar of Dreams*, p. 11) This statement makes the reader curious as to what he will find out in the second chapter. At the end of the second chapter, "Papa didn't answer. He just looked distracted. And that's when I knew something was definitely bothering Papa." (*A Jar of Dreams*, p. 21) This makes the reader wonder what is bothering Papa. In addition, at the end of chapter five, "I looked at the clock and thought in just one more hour I would meet Aunt Waka at last." (*A Jar of Dreams*, p. 48) The reader is curious to find out what Aunt Waka looks like because no fewer than five chapters have been about her anticipated arrival. At the end of chapter six, there is another reference to Aunt Waka. "But I was busy thinking about Aunt Waka and how different she seemed from Mama. It wasn't just because she'd come from Japan. It was something else.

Something that made her seem sort of special. I wasn't sure what it was but then I had all summer to find out." (*A Jar of Dreams*, p. 59) Again the reader is led to be curious about Aunt Waka and what makes her so special. This device makes the sequence of actions in the story flow smoothly and keeps the reader interested in what happens in the following chapters. We see Rinko trying to understand and solve her problem by her own actions. No one but Rinko can come to her own understanding. At the end of each chapter we have Rinko's thoughts with a promise of something interesting to follow. Each new chapter grows naturally out of the previous scene.

In addition, the ending of the book takes us back to the novel's first paragraph. The first words of the book are: "I never thought one small lady from Japan could make such a big difference in my life, but she did." (*A Jar of Dreams*, p. 3) The last lines state: "I stood there a long time watching Aunt Waka's ship going further and further away from me, until finally my blue streamer was all unrolled and went flying off into the summer sky." (*A Jar of Dreams*, p. 131) The moral fable of the book is contained in the advice Aunt Waka offers Rinko just before she leaves. "Rinko, don't ever be ashamed of who you are,' she said.'Just be the best person you can. Believe in your own worth. And someday I know you'll be able to feel proud of yourself, even the part of you that's different ... the part that's Japanese.'" (*A Jar of Dreams*, p. 125) This moral, however, is not intended for Japanese readers alone. As Uchida says, "Though my books have been about Japanese, I always hope they enlarge the reader's understanding about the human condition. It's important that we all take pride in our cultural experience, so we don't lose that feeling of the community of man." (*San Francisco Examiner*, p. S-6) The structure of *A Jar of Dreams* is tightly controlled to convey Uchida's fable, which addresses her Japanese-American readers with special urgency but speaks to others as well.

Journey to Topaz and *Journey Home* are like one long book divided into two equal parts. Together they form a circular strategy, a trip to Topaz and a return home. Other children's books have used this structural strategy. At the beginning and end of her adventures in *The Wizard of Oz*, Dorothy finds herself in her own bed. Likewise Scrooge in Dickens's *A Christmas Carol* finds himself in his own bed after his various adventures. The structural motion is circular. There is no turning point, but at the end of the novel the main character has learned something he hasn't known before. A change has occurred in his inner being as a result of the adventures he has undergone. Likewise the basic plot structure of *Journey to Topaz, Journey Home,* and *A Jar of Dreams* is circular in order to serve Uchida's moral fable. There are also parallel plot lines. All the main characters experience physical burdens but undergo internal changes as well. This pattern produces a very positive affirmation. In *Journey to Topaz,* Yuki returns from her camp and sees the world in a new way. "It is as though she were seeing the whole world with a new eye. The colors seemed brighter, the air seemed fresher, the sounds sharper. It was as though she had climbed out of a cocoon and suddenly discovered the sun." (*Journey to Topaz,* p. 149) In *Journey Home* Yuki realizes, "They'd all come home at last, even Ken. And Yuki knew that everything was going to be all right. She'd finally came home too." (*Journey Home,* p. 131) In *A Jar of Dreams* Rinko fully appreciates her Aunt Waka: "and then it happened, like a light bulb had been switched on in my head. At that very minute I finally knew what made Aunt Waka seem so special. She was exactly the kind of person she was telling me to be. She believed in herself and she liked herself. But mostly, I guess she was proud of who she was." (*A Jar of Dreams,* p. 125) In all these stories the main character moves from emotional insecurity to a stronger realization of self-esteem. This is the message that Uchida wants to convey to her early adolescent readers.

Although the books have many similar structural elements, each has its own intrinsic message based on the particular problem it poses. The three books show Yuki at different stages of growth. In *Journey to Topaz,* it is quite frightening for Yuki to be sent to a relocation camp. However, Uchida's message is that even in the worst places one can strive to be happy. As Lee Wyndham points out, "Children can thrive under the most adverse physical and social conditions if the home atmosphere is happy." (Wyndham, p. 68) Thus Yuki's resolution grows out of this particular problem. In *Journey Home*, the Sakane family faces different obstacles. When they return to Berkeley they face hostility from their neighbors. The book focuses on Yuki, who suffers from discrimination, and on Ken, who learns to cope with his disillusionment and bitterness. However, as a result of their problems, the characters reach another stage in their development. In *Jar of Dreams* Rinko [Yuki] grows significantly trying to determine her self-worth. As she says at the end of the novel, "All I could do was just stand there straight and tall." (*A Jar of Dreams*, p. 130) Thus, the three books show Yuki at different stages of self-esteem. For Yuki each stage is an important step in the progress toward inner strength.

It is true that from an aesthetic or structural point of view the three books are quite simple. However, we should keep in mind that the books were written for eight to twelve-year-olds. Uchida's style fits her purpose. Like many educators, she believes that the best way for young people to gain a deeper understanding of other ethnic groups is to read about them. As the reader travels with Yuki step by step through each of the three books, he more fully shares in the stages of Yuki's growth.

Uchida's best-known book, *Picture Bride*, is the story of the mother. In this novel, which is written for adults, we don't see the mother from the daughter's eyes as a strong and supportive person; rather we discover the portrait of a woman, first as an innocent girl, then as a young woman struggling to remain faithful to her husband, and finally as a lonely but mature woman.

In this novel the mother first comes to the States as a picture bride. A picture bride is a woman who agrees to marry a man just by looking at his picture. Arranged marriages have existed for centuries in Asian countries. As late as the 1940s this custom was acceptable and convenient, and perhaps the only way an Asian could marry in the States. The man usually saved for several years so he could send the transportation expenses to his future bride. Hana, a beautiful and healthy young girl from a small village in Japan, decides to come to marry Taro, an older man who now lives in California. When she sees him for the first time, she notices his kind eyes but does not fall in love with him. She is equally disappointed at his small store and bleak economic situation. To her, America isn't the golden mountain that she dreamed of. She notices a younger man, Yamaka, with whom she can't help falling in love. This causes much inner stress and pain for Hana. When she first sees Yamaka, "she realized she had never before talked with a man with whom she felt so completely at ease .... She longed to tell him what joy she felt in simply being close enough to touch him. For the first time since she had come from Japan, she felt intensely alive." (*Picture Bride*, p. 39) A friend, Henry Toda, senses her feelings. "She caught Henry Toda's eye. In an instant, she knew that he understood everything." (*Picture Bride*, p. 46) Hana is quite embarrassed and ashamed. She tries desperately to fight her feelings and resist temptation. Although she is strongly tempted, she does not betray Taro. "The fact that she had successfully curbed Yamaka's passion as well as her own seemed somehow to purge the guilt that pricked at her so constantly .... Now, however, she knew that Taro did not believe her. She had lost his respect and trust, perhaps causing the loss of one of his closest friends. Whatever love Taro might still have would now be tempered by doubt." (*Picture Bride*, p. 53) It is interesting to note that Hana, due to her strict cultural upbringing, feels such guilt although in fact she is quite innocent. The problem with Yamaka is only resolved when he dies of illness.

The overall structure of the book is that of an artistic biography. The chapters are structured around landmarks in Hana's life. Hana's relationships with her daughter, Mary, and a mentally ill student, Nishima, serve as subplots. The thirty-five chapters of *Picture Bride* cover twenty-five years and include the highlights in Hana's life such as her arrival in the States, her marriage, her love for another man, her life as a housewife, her relationship with her daughter, and the death of her husband. Instead of chapter titles Uchida uses dates. This device gives the portrait more historical significance. The first nine chapters focus on only one year, 1917-1918, in which we witness Hana's life as a bride. As the title might indicate, these experiences are crucial to Hana's growth, so

Uchida devotes nine chapters to this one year. Subsequent chapters deal with longer periods of time until Hana is a mature adult.

The frame of this book is also that of a journey. Not only is it a physical journey from a small village in Japan to California, it is a journey of positive inner growth. Like such canonical figures as Virginia Woolf and Henry James, Uchida writes about the recesses of the mind although she does not use stream of consciousness. She allows the reader to share Hana's inner conflicts and choices. At the beginning of the novel we come to understand why Hana chooses to leave Japan and become a picture bride. We sympathize when, confronted with an overwhelming love for Yamaka, Hana struggles to control her thoughts. "She beseeched Buddha and Taro's Christian God to purify her soul at the start of this next year in her new life. She tried to hold on to the good thoughts, but too many other thoughts crowded them out." (*Picture Bride*, p. 41) At the end of the novel we are in a good position to appreciate Hana decision to stand tall despite her circumstances. The experiences we share with Hana are those that most picture brides encountered. As Uchida points out, "they [picture brides] may seem very non-assertive, but they were women of real strength." (*San Francisco Examiner*, p. S-6) As Kenji observes, " [Picture brides] each crossed an ocean alone to come to this country, and they're going to survive the future with the same strength and spirit. I know it." (*Picture Bride*, p. 216) Like Yuki, Rinko, and Ken, Hana confronts internal as well as physical realities as well. Both realities are linked structurally to convey a moral fable in which Uchida illustrates her principal values.

As was pointed out earlier, there are parallel plot lines in the first three books and similar incidents in all four books. In *Picture Bride* incidents from the other books are repeated from the mother's point of view. For example, hostile neighbors are portrayed through Hana's eyes. "Hana became so fearful of offending her neighbors, she was even careful about where and how she hung her laundry. She wondered if they objected to the diapers that fluttered on her line each day, and she took pains to hang any undergarments out of sight from their neighbors' windows." (*Picture Bride*, p. 69) In this story we don't see the strong, consistently calm mother Yuki or Rinko sees. In addition, as in the previous stories there are unpleasant incidents of discrimination against the Japanese. Four white men visit Hana's home one day. "'We'll come right to the point,' a tall red-headed man said without bothering to sit down. 'There've been some complaints from the neighborhood about having Japanese on this block.'" (*Picture Bride*, p. 66) Taro and Hana do not move, however, and the neighbors come to tolerate them. Hana seems to voice the author's thoughts about discrimination: "'Peril?' Hana asked incredulously. 'We Japanese are a peril to this enormous country?' It was beyond belief." (*Picture Bride*, p. 63) Mary also encounters discrimination when she goes swimming at the public pool and is told by strangers that she wouldn't enjoy swimming there. Mary becomes so intimidated that when she goes for a haircut she calls first to ask if they cut Japanese hair.

As in the other stories, there are kind Americans who befriend the family. Ellen Davis is such a person. Hana goes to her house once a week to help clean the house. "Ellen Davis was touched by the sacrifices of Hana's people. She knew how each family struggled simply to exist, and yet they seemed always ready to help one another when the need arose .... They were proud, hardworking people, and Ellen Davis was outraged at the discrimination heaped on them with the sanction of law." (*Picture Bride*, p. 94) Ellen gives Taro a job painting her house. In many ways like the Olssens, Jamiesons, and Nelsons of previous novels, Ellen is a more realistic version of the kinder Americans who populate Uchida's stories. However, Ellen is described more fully in this longer novel. She asks Hana to eat with her and even lets Hana use her late son's napkin ring. Ellen also provides jobs for Hana and Taro.

The recurring elements are bleaker and more realistic than in the other books. In *Journey Home* when Yuki breaks her mother's favorite vase, Mama comforts Yuki by saying, "Look at it this way, Yuki. Maybe my vase was broken in order to spare your brother. Maybe it was destroyed in place of something happening to Ken." (*Journey Home*, p. 31) This incident serves two functions. It reveals Mama's and Uchida's positive attitudes and it also foretells future events in the story. The incident of the broken plate is retold in *Picture Bride*. "Hana broke a plate as she was washing the supper dishes. It was a bad omen. She got some glue and tried to piece it together. If I can fix it then Kiyoshi San will live, she told herself. But the plate fell apart even before the glue could dry." (*Picture Bride*, p. 58) Unlike the incident in *Journey Home*, this one depicts the mother breaking the plate. In this incident the plate is not broken to substitute for Ken's life; rather it foretells the death of Kiyoshi Yamaka.

In the earlier books the characterization of Yuki and Rinko is very similar. In *Picture Bride* Mary is an older version. We see Mary as a teenager and then as a young woman. It is a difficult time for Mary to grow up. "For some years now, Mary had known that her Japanese face denied her certain privileges. White people had their own special world, and the Japanese Americans were not a part of it, except perhaps as servants, day workers, gardeners or cooks. When she went to the City Plunge with her friends one day she was told, "'We don't think you'll enjoy swimming here.'" (*Picture Bride*, p. 131) The mother and daughter also grow apart. The mother never learns enough English to communicate with her daughter and the daughter cannot speak Japanese. "Hana knew very well why she and Mary were becoming strangers. They were gradually losing the means of communicating with one another. Hana had never insisted that Mary go to Japanese Language School as some of the Nisei children had done, and she herself had not progressed far in studying English." (*Picture Bride*, p. 135) Thus, Hana and her daughter do not have a close relationship as Yuki or Rinko has with her mother.

Mary elopes with an American and this causes her parents much pain. The Japanese are strict about interracial marriages and the elopement as well as the fact Mary marries a white person causes great anguish for her parents. Mary, however, feels free of her Japanese background. "Now she was Mary Cantelli, Mrs. Joseph Cantelli. She had discarded her old life and everything she detested about it. Now she need never again be humiliated because her name was Takeda.

Only the thought of her parents flickered in her mind like a bothersome insect that would not leave." (*Picture Bride*, p. 146) At the end of the novel, Mary tries to effect a reconciliation by asking her mother to live with her, but the mother declines. This more somber but realistic conclusion is anticipated by other unpretty events. The two main male characters in the novel, Taro and his friend Toda, are both killed. Toda is murdered by a drunken stranger one night on his farm, while Taro is killed by a guard who thinks that Taro is trying to escape although he is only looking for arrowheads near the fence. Altogether, *Picture Bride* offers a world apparently much darker than Uchida previously rendered.

The last scene consists of two widows walking hand in hand down a dusty road. "[Sumiko] saw Hana and Kiku deep in conversation as they walked down the dusty road. They did not even seem aware of the murky gathering of clouds in the sky or feel the ominous gusts of the hot, trembling wind. They did not know that by the time they walked to Hana's barrack at the opposite end of camp, another dust storm would be coursing over the desert sands, enveloping all of Topaz in its white fury." (*Picture Bride* p. 216) The key images, "dust storm" and "white fury," seem to symbolize the discrimination that the two widows will continue to encounter.

Nonetheless, this last paragraph also points up the resilience of these Japanese American women. The book is dedicated "in memory of those brave women from Japan who travelled far, who endured, and who prevailed." Despite the novel's "white fury," the reader is led to believe that somehow the two widows will survive and manage. As in the earlier books, Uchida ends by stressing inner strength. The main characters develop this positive vision as a result of the experiences they undergo. Written for adults, *Picture Bride* is a more realistic and somber version of the earlier works, but its affirmations are therefore more compelling.

The values that Uchida stresses are American as well as Japanese. Nineteenth-century poets such as Longfellow, Emerson, and Bryant voiced similar aspirations in their poems. Uchida's heroines, especially Rinko's mother, Aunt Waka, and Hana, are strong women. Despite their circumstances they are positive and disciplined. These women are Uchida's role models. Uchida's moral fable in all her stories is consistent with her conviction that one should hope for a better tomorrow. As Uchida says, "Today, so much of the world is dehumanizing. And a child is aware of a lot of ugliness in this life. I think a child needs hope. That's the main difference between adult and children's books ... you always leave children with a sense of hope." (*San Francisco Examiner*, p. S-6) As it happens, this same desire to end with a "sense of hope" can be seen in Uchida's one adult novel as well. Perhaps nothing else marks her so clearly as a second-generation Japanese American.

Thus, Uchida's contribution is significant. Her purpose is not only to entertain her readers but to influence their thinking. Her tightly controlled stories also make a contribution to interracial understanding. As Whitney points out, "Ethnic themes in books for young people have had a strong influence on changing views in our society." (Whitney, p. 141) Uchida would agree, as when she mentions that "the need to break down racial stereotypes in children's stories is especially urgent now that increasing numbers of Asian children and their families are immigrating here." (*San Francisco Examiner*, p.S-6) Books like Uchida's, I am sure, do add to cultural understanding. Some readers might find it distasteful to read about Japanese internment camps. However, I think such honesty appeals to today's young readers. Furthermore, it isn't the subject that really matters but how the author treats the subject. In Uchida's case it is always in a positive as well as an artistic manner.

There is an appealing universality about children's needs and aspirations. Novels such as *Tom Sawyer*, *Heidi*, and *Little Women* have entertained young adults all over the world for years. Although Rinko and Yuki are Japanese characters, they can stand next to Tom, Heidi, Meg, Jo, Beth, and Amy. To a considerable extent, human nature is the same the world over. The characters and settings may be different but the commonality of experience allows the non-Japanese American reader to understand and take pleasure in the book. Thus we understand *Heidi* and *Bury My Heart at Wounded Knee* although we are not Swiss or American Indian.

In the field of Asian American literature, Uchida's contribution is especially significant because there are only a few writers of children's literature. Chinese-American Lawrence Yep has written books about growing up in America and Kim Yong Ik has written about his childhood in a Korean village. Uchida has written more such books, however, and more successful ones than any of her peers. Whether writing for children, adolescents, or adults, Uchida offers a convincing positive vision. In each story her main characters are overcomers. This is the moral fable and design that Uchida has drawn carefully from her own experiences.

Chapter Six

Maxine Hong Kingston:
The Writer as Warrior

Maxine Hong Kingston's first novel is a triumph for Asian American literature. Presently, a required text at such universities as U.C. Berkeley and U.C. Santa Barbara, *The Woman Warrior* (1976) is a book in which Kingston brings together many diverse materials and presents them in a strikingly original form. It addresses more than one audience and brings them together, as Asian American materials are presented in such a way as to allow the Asian American response to be all but indistinguishable from the American one.

Nonetheless, *The Woman Warrior* has received conflicting criticism about its purpose and significance. According to Mary Gordon of the *New York Times*, "*The Woman Warrior* was a brilliantly realized attempt to understand herself in relation to Chinese women, mythical and actual." (Gordon, p. 24) This explanation makes the book seem a somewhat private pursuit. Elaine Kim, associate professor at U.C. Berkeley, has reached a similar conclusion: "*The Woman Warrior* is an attempt to sort out what being a Chinese American means." (Kim, "Visions," p. 147) Kim further points out that "*The Woman Warrior* is about women but it is primarily about the Chinese American's attempt to sort fact from fantasy in order to come to terms with the paradoxes that shape her life as a member of a racial minority group in America." ("Visions," p. 154) Gordon and Kim define the purpose of this book in terms of a personal quest. I disagree with their explanations, for I don't think the novel is an exercise in self-therapy. In addition, the word "attempt" suggests a result somewhat short of success. If this book is "an attempt to sort out fantasy from reality," then the author sounds a bit schizophrenic. I hope to show that the fantasy in the novel has a definite thematic and structural purpose.

I also disagree with Linda Sledge's and Ruth Hsaio's classifications. Sledge argues that *The Woman Warrior* fits the category of ethnobiography. "In Maxine Kingston's *Woman Warrior* ... the history of one girl and her family is identified with the history of an immigrant race spanning old and new worlds. Kingston is simultaneously a participant in her race's history and the storytelling direction of those events. She speaks with the voices of assorted legendary and real-life persons: the voices of ancient heroes and heroines: the ceremonial voice of the family." (Sledge, p. 43) Sledge's explanation contradicts Gordon's. Instead of a personal attempt at self-realization, *The Woman Warrior* is defined as representing the several voices of the Chinese immigrant race. Sledge's assertion is rather like saying that Kingston's family and experiences are those of all Chinese Americans. The characterizations in this book do not support this notion. Brave Orchid, the mother, is definitely a unique character. Anju, the daughter who narrates part of the novel, is not a stereotypical character either. Indeed, Kingston relies very little on what is "typical."

Hsaio calls *The Woman Warrior* a psychological novel. "It contains truths that defy the logic of the outer world but are true, nevertheless. Writing from this inner perspective she is giving us a psychological novel like Henry Roth's *Call It Sleep*." (Hsaio, p. 189) I would also quarrel with this statement. *Call It Sleep* is a long, long novel about a Jewish boy growing up in Brooklyn. It has a logical plot and traditional character development. Indeed, its entire form is traditional whereas *The Woman Warrior* interweaves five different stories. Although *The Woman Warrior* does have psychological elements, the legends and historical myths do not fit the category of a psychological novel. In addition, unlike *Call It Sleep*, Kingston's novel focuses on several women at different times in their lives.

The fact that this book is about five women has led several critics to conclude that it is a feminist novel. Nellie Wong emphasizes the feminist point of view: "Indeed, *The Woman Warrior* is written from a feminist perspective .... Her feminist perspective is an outgrowth of her literary impulses to relate ... what she has heard from her mother's talk story ... and ... what she has experienced .... Maxine threads the theme of female namelessness, voicelessness, and powerlessness throughout the book." (Wong, pp. 46-47) It seems evident that the ethnobiographer and the feminist have classified the book according to their own perspectives.

Kingston herself denies that *The Woman Warrior* is a feminist or an ethnic book. In an interview with Henry Allen of the *Washington Post* she states, "I don't think I'm only a feminist writer, or an ethnic writer, but I'm writing at a time when feminism and ethnic studies are popular, so people find that in my writing." (Allen, D4) Elsewhere she has been even more explicit in rejecting a feminist approach to her book even though she acknowledges that she is a feminist. In her interview with Arturo Islas she says, "I have always been a feminist but feminism is just one modern political stance .... One has to have an even larger vision. I don't think that my writing would limit itself to whatever is politically useful." (Yalom, p. 16) Thus it is hard to believe that she wrote *The Woman Warrior* to promote feminism. At the MLA convention in San Francisco in December 1991, she said that if she were to rewrite the episode of Fa Mu Lan, she would have the warrior return home and change into a beautiful woman rather than remain a warrior.

It is difficult, in fact, to classify this book in any neat category. *The Woman Warrior* stands by itself in its theme and structure. It has mixed genes or elements. It is like chop suey. Chop Suey is not an authentic Chinese dish but an Americanized version of a Chinese dish. The mixed ingredients are measured carefully to satisfy the American appetite. The "cook" is an American who has learned how to cook from a Chinese cookbook although she doesn't understand the recipes completely. Thus her dish satisfies the American appetite but contains some secret ingredients that only the Chinese are familiar with. By analogy, to analyze this novel fully the critic should have some background in Asian customs.

Yet the novel can be read on many different levels and most American critics agree that it is very successful despite their conflicting interpretations. That Kingston's novel is acclaimed by well-known critics shows that many qualified readers find this book suitably addressed to the American public. To understand the Asian materials is to appreciate the sources of this success and perhaps to grasp Kingston's meaning a bit more firmly than her more general American audience has managed to date.

Like the ingredients in chop suey, the details in this Asian American novel have a unique flavor. As Paul Gray says, "Art has intervened here. The stories may or may not be transcripts of actual experience. They are, unquestionably, triumphant journeys of imagination through a desolation of spirit." (Gray, p. 29) Art has transformed Kingston's imagination into dynamic stories with details so piercing and powerful that one can feel the scenes long after the last page is read.

How does Kingston achieve this effect? The first important step in unraveling this book is to separate fantasy from reality. Hsaio points out that "these legends, fairytales, ghost stories, historical narrative biographies of legendary figures either appear in chapter length form or in the middle of a modern incident." (Hsaio, p. 199) Kingston herself admits that her narrative pattern is hard to understand. She compares herself to an outlaw knotmaker. "His version of the story may be better than mine because of its bareness, not twisted into designs .... There was one knot so complicated that it blinded the knotmaker. Finally an emperor outlawed this cruel knot, and the nobles could not order it anymore. If I had lived in China, I would have been an outlaw knotmaker." (Kingston, pp. 189-190) This metaphor is appropriate for Kingston, for *The Woman Warrior* tells stories within stories.

Indeed, to overtake Kingston at her task is like untying a very complicated knot. The first step is to distinguish the use of the word "fantasy" as a generic label from the elements of fantasy. Critics have stated that the book is an attempt to "sort out fantasy from fact," for in the *Woman Warrior* there are elements of fantasy, biography, and fiction. The book has also been called the best nonfiction published in 1976 by the

National Book Critics Circle. However, this complicated book should not be classified as straightforward nonfiction. There are so many elements drawn from different genres that it would be wrong to define it as belonging to one category. Sheldon Sacks in *Fiction and the Shape of Belief* makes a strong point in distinguishing the elements of satire from the definition of satire as a genre: "If we are aware that the term 'satire' is being used in a flexible sense, such critique may prove illuminating. But from the moment we confuse the everyday use of the term with its uses in discriminating a literary type according to an informing principle, chaos results." (Sacks, p. 12) Kim and others have used the word "fantasy" in a popular sense rather than using it to identify a literary type.

My task here is not to pursue a detailed study of the novel's several elements, to classify or "define" *The Woman Warrior*, but simply to point out that the shape of this novel accommodates a belief that is complex and seemingly paradoxical. This is in the contemporary tradition. Bernard A. Schopen notes in his doctoral dissertation *The Aesthetics of Ambiguity: The Novels of John Updike*, "For Updike the art of the novel is a continuous and deliberate effort to seek out new forms." (Schopen, p. 39), and I think this is what Kingston is doing as well. Kingston has skillfully created a form to accommodate her complex theme. As Kingston has said, "I learned to make my mind large, as the universe is large, so that there is room for paradoxes." (Kim, *Asian American Literature* p. 20) Kingston has also said that writing is an "emotional process." (Hsaio, p. 185) Emotion and reason often do not go together. Where there is emotion there is also paradox. However, the artist has definitely given the book its meaningful shape. This book is not an emotional outpouring of free association. The discussion which follows may at times seem repetitious and circular, but this is due to the fact that many points and details overlap.

There is a definite organization to the novel. Each of the five chapters is about one of the principal characters. The characters are divided into the strong and the weak. Brave Orchid and Fa Mu Lan are the strong characters, Moon Orchid and the No Name Woman the weak characters. Anju, the daughter, possesses both strong and weak characteristics.

The daughter imagines herself to be the woman warrior, but she is also identified with the Quiet Girl. Indeed, the five chapters function to illustrate the various feminine models Anju knows from her family. The five characters model strong and weak traits that consciously or unconsciously are a part of Anju's character. Each chapter offers Anju's descriptions of and reflections on one of these characters. This process is very important because at the end Anju reaches her conviction to follow the strong models, these models presented in chapters two and three. Fa Mu Lan, the woman warrior herself, is the subject of chapter two, "White Tigers." She is the fabled woman who learns to be a great warrior from two elderly people in some imaginary highlands. She uses her knowledge and skill gained from fifteen years of training to form an army and overthrow the cruel ruling class of China, thus avenging oppressions, grievances, and deaths experienced by her family and friends. For Anju, Fa Mu Lan is impressive. She imagines herself to be the warrior.

The main character in the third chapter, "Shaman," is the mother, Brave Orchid, who as her name indicates is brave, strong, and diligent. She is a doctor in China before coming to live in the United States. When China is at war with Japan, Brave Orchid sets up a hospital in a cave and helps the injured. In 1939 she comes to the United States to join her husband. She is already in her forties when she arrives, but she has six more children after she is forty-five. She works from 6 a.m. to midnight every day in her laundry to help feed her children. She also saves enough money to bring her younger sister, Moon Orchid, to the States. As Suzanne Juhasz notes, "Brave Orchid's heroism ... identifies her with the woman warrior, because her success, like the warrior's is based on powers of the imagination." (Juhasz, p. 181) Brave Orchid's imagination reveals another side to her character. She is full of stories she shares with her children. According to Juhasz, "the factual and fantastic tales of Brave Orchid combine to make her a complete person in her daughter's eyes, a person with a separate identity both to be proud of and of necessity to reject, to move beyond." (Juhasz, p. 181) It seems that the mother uses these tales as examples of virtue.

Kim points out that the stories of the No Name Woman and
Fu Ma Lan deeply impress Anju. Yet these two stories are
about two extremely different women. Kim describes them as
"paradoxical and dualistic, setting the tone for the entire
book." (Kim, "Visions," p. 150) The tale of the No Name
woman is told to Anju by her mother to deter Anju from
following the wrong example. Fu Ma Lan's story is told to
Anju because the mother wants Anju to follow the more
positive path. Her mother's value judgments are those of old
China. The daughter is able to question those judgments. In
fact, the tone of the chapter implies that the daughter is
sympathetic to her dead aunt. Thus, Brave Orchid is characterized as a strong person, but she is limited to her own
perceptions. Brave Orchid likes to sing the story of the
woman warrior to her daughter. The narrator in "White
Tigers" states, "After I grew up, I heard the chant of Fa Mu
Lan, the girl who took her father's place in battle. Instantly I
remembered that as a child I had followed my mother about
the house, the two of us singing about how Fa Mu Lan fought
gloriously and returned alive from war to settle in the village."
(Kingston, p. 24) To Brave Orchid the woman warrior should
be a role model for her daughter.

After two very positive models in chapters two and three,
Kingston turns to decisively weaker ones. Indeed, the first
relatively weaker model is projected in chapter one where the
No Name Woman is a victim. Kingston returns to this kind of
figure in chapter four, "At the Western Palace," where she
deals with Moon Orchid, Brave Orchid's sister. Moon
Orchid's husband leaves the village to come to the United
States to study. Although he sends her money, he never sends
for her. When she is in her sixties, her older sister Brave
Orchid sends her enough money to come to the States. Moon
Orchid tries to help her sister but she is rather non-produc-
tive. She also drives her relatives up the wall, as her old
Chinese ways clash with the American ways of her relatives to
provide the reader with some humorous moments. For example, "Sometimes when the girls were reading or watching television, she crept up behind them with a comb and tried to
smooth their hair, but they shook their heads, and they turned

and fixed her with those eyes." (Kingston, p. 154) At other times, "She hovered over a child who was reading." (Kingston, p. 155) These examples provide dramatic irony. Moon Orchid thinks that she is being very helpful and does not realize that she is disturbing the girls. The American reader can see that Moon Orchid is really irritating the girls; however, for a Chinese reader Moon Orchid is being very concerned and thoughtful about her nieces' needs. Here, as in other incidents, Kingston communicates how Anju is feeling by exposing the reader to Anju's thoughts. Anju thinks and speaks like an American so the American audience can clearly understand what she is saying. However, in this case an Asian American can perhaps understand Moon Orchid's point of view as well, although Moon Orchid's thoughts are not stated in this incident. Kingston does not so much invite us to adopt an American or an Asian American perspective as to appreciate the contrast between them. As Hsaio points out, "Through imaginative transcendence the ordinary incident becomes a fable of the impossibility of communication." (Hsaio, p. 194) Indeed, the generation gap as well as cultural misunderstandings make communication between the two generations very difficult at best.

Brave Orchid wants to take Moon Orchid to see her husband, but Moon Orchid, a very timid and frightened woman, at first refuses to go. Already married to another woman, the husband refuses to do anything with Moon Orhcid although he promises to send her more money. Her husband treats her cruelly when he sees her again. "He turned to Moon Orchid, 'You can't talk to them. You can barely talk to me.' Moon Orchid was so ashamed, she hid her hands over her face." (Kingston, p. 178) She realizes how old and useless she is to him when she meets him. This realization is what leaves her in a mental asylum for the rest of her life. Its humor notwithstanding, there is a lot of pain in this chapter.

Chapter five, "A Song for a Barbarian Reed Pipe," explains how Anju grew up. Growing up in Stockton, California, was not easy for the very shy narrator. Although born in the States in 1940, she does not feel like an American: "During the first silent year I spoke to no one at school, did not ask before going to the lavatory and flunked kindergarten." (Kingston, p. l92) She hates to talk. "A telephone call makes my throat bleed and takes up that day's courage .... I'm getting better now, though." (Kingston, p. 191) The narrator hates her American school whwere she doesn't talk for three years. She is miserable at school and her black paintings reflect her sadness, despair, and fears. She feels better in a Chinese school she attends after her regular school. The Chinese school is filled with loud Chinese voices, screams, and yells.

Like her mother, the daughter perceives everyone as ghosts. She calls Negro students "Black ghosts" and describes the Japanese students as "noisy and tough." Apparently, she sees others as stereotypes. There are also times at school when she is laughed at but does not know it. "I drank out of a toy saucer when the water spilled out of the cup and everybody laughed, pointing at me, so I did it some more. I didn't know that Americans don't drink out of saucers." (Kingston, p. 192) Anju thinks that her classmates are laughing because they are friendly and approving, whereas the reader (both American and Asian American) realizes that everyone is in reality laughing at her. In this chapter we see Anju having a miserable childhood. The negative model in this chapter is the youthful Anju herself. At the end of the book, however, Anju decides to follow more positive models. Indeed, she is the only character who changes or grows in the novel.

"A Song for a Barbarian Reed Pipe" includes the story of the Quiet Girl. Anju hates this classmate who never talks in school. Perhaps she hates the girl's quietness because she herself has always been so quiet at school. The Quiet Girl represents all that Anju wants to avoid, so Anju is threatened by this girl. Anju becomes irrationally angry when she finds herself one afternoon alone with the girl in the school bathroom. "' You are going to talk,' I said, my voice steady and normal as it is when talking to the familiar, the weak, and the small. 'I am going to make you talk, you sissy-girl.'" (Kingston, p. 204) Full of anger she starts abusing this girl who just sits there quiet and afraid. Anju starts jeering at her: "Look at you, snot streaming down your nose, and you won't say a word to stop it. You're such a nothing." (Kingston, p.

207) Anju hates the girl's smooth, white skin and thin neck. She also despises the pastel colors the Quiet Girl is wearing. Anju continues pinching the girl's cheeks and tormenting her psychologically and physically. "If you don't talk, you can't have a personality .... You think somebody's going to care of you all your stupid life? You think you'll always have your big sister? You think somebody's going to marry you, is that it? Well, you're not the type that gets dates, let alone gets married." (Kingston, p. 210)   The confrontation exhausts Anju. "'I don't understand why you won't say just one word,' I cried, clenching my teeth. My knees were shaking, and I hung on to her hair to stand up." (Kingston, p. 210) It is interesting to note that Anju says she doesn't understand why the Quiet Girl won't talk although Anju herself didn't talk the first three years of her schooling.

Thus the strong and weak women are juxtaposed for the sake of contrast. In addition the real persons have their shadows. For example, Brave Orchid's shadow is Fa Mu Lan, Moon Orchid's is the No Name Woman, and Anju's is the Quiet Girl. As mentioned before, Anju possesses both strong and weak traits and so becomes a bridge between the strong and the weak. The process is Hegelian. This movement toward synthesis applies not only to the novel's characterizations but also its form. The shape of belief in this novel is partly Chinese and partly American, like its narrator, Anju. The synthesis is not only Hegelian but also Chinese. Hegel's ascending stages move from thesis to antithesis to synthesis. Likewise the concept of the yin and yang moves from contrast to synthesis. The Chinese have always viewed the world as a synthesis of two opposing forces. Nineteenth century American writers reflect similar forms of synthesis in their writings. For example, Emerson uses the "Each and All" premise in his definitions of a seashell and the American scholar. Likewise, Kingston uses the synthesis of the yin and yang in a broad sense to shape her unique message.

The mother/daughter relationship helps bring about the formal synthesis. I don't think that the daughter sees her mother as a negative influence. Together mother and daughter sing the legend of Fa Mu Lan. "Instantly I remembered that as a child I had followed my mother about the house, the two of us singing about how Fa Mu Lan fought gloriously and returned alive from war to settle in the village." (Kingston, p. 24) The relationsip between mother and daughter is close despite some communication problems. Hsaio points out that "centuries of traditions and customs intercept communication between the immigrant and American born." (Hsaio, p. 195) The shouting matches are a result of misunderstanding between mother and daughter. However, as Anju becomes older and reflects on the different models she finally acknowledges her mother's influence. The mother becomes Anju's final model. As Kingston once said, "My mother is the creative one— the one with the visions and the stories to tell, I'm the technician. She is the great inspiration. I never realized it until I finished the book." (Robertson, p. 26)

The second step in untying the narrative knot is to identify the narrative patterns. Juhasz points out that the first three stories are about the mother or told by her and the two final stories are by or about the daughter: "Complex is really a better word for the various kinds of narrative movements that taken together reflect the dynamics of the mother-daughter relationship. The move to individualize and the move to connect both arise from the essential attachment." (Juhasz, p. 177) She concludes that "Within each of the stories other movements occur in alternating patterns, maintaining the necessary tension between separation and connection." (Juhasz, p. 177) This tension between the mother and daughter reinforces the tension between the imaginary and real worlds.

Kingston once stated that the book is arranged according to her brain patterns. She imagines herself as a legendary warrior, then jumps *in medias res* to a scene in her own childhood. Fearful scenes of ghosts are mixed with scenes from real life. However, her method is not like Joyce's stream of consciousness. Kingston's pattern is not a cluster of free associations but an arrangement of definite conclusions. At the end of each chapter, Kingston draws a conclusion about the narration. The summaries at the end of each of her chapters give the reader the chapter's main points or "lesson."

These lessons prove that Kingston is an artist with an audience in mind. In other words, Kingston is not simply sorting out fantasy and reality for herself. She is writing for an American audience, and she wants to make sure the reader understands.

Let us examine the endings of the chapters. At the end of chapter one she states, "My aunt haunts me — her ghost drawn to me because now after fifty years of neglect, I alone devote pages of pages to her." (Kingston, p. 19) Here Kingston begins the process of reflecting on each of the models. Anju wonders why she is the only person remembering this aunt. The No Name Aunt drowned herself after being beaten by the villagers for becoming pregnant without a husband.   The injustice done to her aunt bothers Anju like a bothersome insect. As a narrator and niece, Anju tries to understand what this story means to her. Why does a story that happened in Asia many years ago bother an Asian American? This starts the process of Anju thinking about herself and the women who have lived before her.

At the end of chapter two, "White Tigers," Kingston again reflects upon the meaning of the experience just rendered. She has just related the story of the woman warrior, Fu Mu Lan. "The swordswoman and I are not so dissimilar. May my people understand the resemblance soon so that I can return to them.   What we have in common are the words at our backs. The ideographs for revenge are 'report a crime' and 'report to five families.' The reporting is the vengeance — not the beheading, not the gutting, but the words. And I have so many words — 'chink' words and 'gook' words too — that they do not fit on my skin." (Kingston, pp. 62-63) Thus, Kingston relates a story about a dead aunt in faraway China and a legend about a Chinese woman warrior, and then rationalizes the significance of these tales.   In a way it is like Thackeray and other novelists who interject their own opinions.   The last paragraph in each of the chapters unlocks the significance of the novel amidst all the narrative complexity.

At the end of chapter three, "Shaman," the narrator states, "I am really a Dragon, as she is a Dragon. both of us born in dragon years.   I am practically a first daughter of a first daughter." (Kingston, p. 127) The "she" in this passage is her mother. That they were both born in the year of the dragon emphasizes their similarities. (Technically, it also means that her mother is forty-eight when Anju is born, as the mother is already in her forties when she arrives in the United States and each of the twelve animals in the Chinese horoscope recurs every twelve years.) The important point is that the daughter feels a strong bond with her mother. The parallels between mother and daughter, warrior and mother, warrior and daughter, and the two aunts give the book much of its cohesiveness.

Chapter four is about Moon Orchid, the aunt, who becomes insane. The ending of this chapter again reveals to us the narrator's main points. The omniscient narrator concludes, "Brave Orchid's daughters decided fiercely that they would never let men be unfaithful to them." (Kingston, p. 186) Unfaithfulness is the cause of Moon Orchid's madness, the chapter's ultimate focus. The daughters witness their aunt's growing illness and are determined not to let any man hurt them. The phrase "never let men be unfaithful" indicates that the daughters realize they have a choice, and their choice is not to follow Moon Orchid's example.

In chapter five the last paragraph ends with the story of a poetess who is captured by the barbarians. She hears the barbarians sing outside her tent every night. One evening she herself starts singing her own song. "Her words seemed to be Chinese, but the barbarians understood their sadness and anger .... She brought her songs back from the savage lands, and one of the three that has been passed down to us is 'Eighteen Stanzas for a Barbarian Reed Pipe,' a song that Chinese sing to their own instruments. It translated well." (Kingston, p. 243) The story of the poetess seems to be a metaphor for her mother's stories Kingston is now translating for the American public. Thus, in each chapter ending Kingston summarizes or metaphorically points up the chapter's significance and reveals clues to her narrative pattern.

To find a pattern is comforting because the narration shifts throughout the book. The shifts are purposeful, however. As Han points out, "She seems always to choose the narrative point of view that best suits the thematic purpose of the story."

(Han, p. 230) Kingston uses the internal first person narration in two of her chapters. The reader is told directly by the narrator what she thinks and feels, which provides an intimacy and a sense of immediacy that third-person narration usually lacks. By using the first person in "White Tigers," Kingston brings immediacy to the story of Fa Mu Lan, a legendary woman warrior. This method makes the character vivid and emphatic. The first-person narration makes a legendary figure in a faraway land more understandable to the American audience. In addition it allows the reader to understand the warrior's effects on Anju and why Anju decides to follow her at the end. By using the "I," the narrator is able to explain the legends to an American audience as the poetess Tsai has translated her Barbarian songs to the Chinese. Anju, the daughter, narrates Fa Mu Lan's story as her own. This narrative technique also makes the fantasy elements more believable. The fantastic and realistic elements become a synthesis of form and fable. The problem that Kim and Gordon encounter in their interpretations is that they identify the "I" in the story with Kingston, but the narrative "I" is a persona and not Kingston. Parts of the story relating to her own childhood may be true, but how can the "I" in the legendary stories also be Kingston?

In "At the Western Palace" the omniscient point of view is used. This allows the reader to understand the thoughts, feelings, and perceptions of all the characters. Brave Orchid's thoughts, Moon Orchid's thoughts, and their Americanized children's thoughts are all revealed, allowing the reader to experience and perhaps understand the family's communication problems as well as their moments of happiness. Omniscience also permits a relatively objective presentation in which the narrator communicates meaning by rendering the scenes so vividly that the reader immediately understands the meaning. This technique is especially crucial in Kingston's handling of the novel's ghosts.

The more objective presentation helps the reader to understand the theme of fear which is artfully arranged in various layers of the book. Kingston uses ghosts thematically to indicate anything that the characters are unfamiliar with or afraid of, often various aspects of American society. For the narrator's family there are white ghosts (Caucasians), black ghosts, and Mexican ghosts. The use of ghosts is sufficently pervasive that the book is appropriately subtitled "Memoirs of a Girlhood among Ghosts." Kingston presents a China and a Chinese American riddled with superstition. Things unfamiliar (such as disease or Japanese airfighters) are explained as supernatural. The unusual events in the hallway of the mother's medical school dorm, the white people in America, and Mexicans are all labeled ghosts. Ghost practically becomes a synonym for people as the ghost metaphor extends throughout the book.

The mother looks on in fear and suspicion at things foreign. She becomes upset when the daughter listens to the teacher ghosts and plays with black ghosts. Her sister, Moon Orchid, is so convinced about the ghosts that she becomes crazy thinking that Mexican ghosts are after her. Had she thought of the Mexicans as people rather than ghosts, she might not have been so fearful of them. Her belief in ghosts contributes to her downfall. Here the concept of ghosts seems to be a metaphor for the old Chinese way of thinking.

Thus the use of ghost implies Kingston's more important judgments. The first appearance of the word "ghost" in the narrative appears in chapter one. The No Name Woman has become a real ghost after her rejection and death. "Always hungry, always needing, she would have to beg food from other ghosts, snatch and steal it from those whose living descendants give them gifts. She would have to fight the ghosts massed at crossroads for the buns a few thoughtful citizens leave to decoy her away from the village and home so that the ancestral spirits could feast unharassed." (Kingston, p. 18) To a western reader this might seem like a piece of interesting imagery; however, for a reader familiar with Asian culture, this is a reference to a special custom for dead relatives. The dead are remembered at the anniversary of their death by a family gathering and feast which they believe the dead come to share. Special food is prepared and placed before the picture of the deceased. The family members bow one by one before the picture. Then the food is left for the dead spirit to enjoy. After ten minutes the family return to eat the ghost's leftovers. In the case of the No Name Aunt no one cares to remember her. The family has rejected her even after her death. Thus, " always hungry, always needing, she would have to beg food from other ghosts." As the dead aunt has no one to remember her on the anniversary of her death, her ghost hopes to snatch a few crumbs from the tables of other ghosts. It is significant that Kingston does not use ghosts only to indicate things foreign but also things Chinese as her aunt is Chinese.

Ghosts are also embedded elsewhere in the novel's structure. Two of the titles have ghostly connotations. The No Name Aunt is a ghost since she is, indeed, dead. "White Tigers" symbolically refers to death as well. The clothes that people wear at a funeral in China are white and white therefore signifies death for the Chinese. The title of the third chapter, "Shaman," is another form of a ghost. In Asia a shaman is a dead person who appears to help someone. Shamanism is an Asian religion that includes the worshiping of dead spirits. In Asia where relatives dead or alive are so cherished this religion is an accepted part of the culture.

The use of ghosts also serves to represent the Chinese point of view, providing a contrast to the daughter's American perspective. As Dasenbrock says, "To understand ghost in *The Woman Warrior*, non-Chinese readers need to understand the Chinese use of the word, which means that we must, momentarily at least, learn to see ourselves as ghosts. As we experience the word, we also experience a perception and a category of thought and in so doing we learn a good deal about Chinese perceptions of us." (Dasenbrock, p. 14) Dasenbrock is saying that all Chinese call foreigners ghosts. This is not a device that Kingston has made up. Rather, Kingston uses this Chinese perception to unify her novel's several stories.

It is also interesting to trace other devices that Kingston uses to help us understand this complex novel. As we have seen, chapter endings are pointed and chapter titles are no less significant. Names are also used to give the reader clues in understanding the nature of the characters, as Kingston follows novelists such as Dickens in naming her characters according to their character traits. The No Name Aunt is so called because no wants to remember her, though I think that she is also so named because she represents all women who have been rejected by society for having conceived before marriage. The Quiet Girl is so called because she represents the typical Chinese girl. Most Chinese girls in the 1940s were extremely quiet at American schools. Brave Orchid, the mother, is indeed characterized as a brave woman. And Moon Orchid, the crazy aunt, is characterized as dreamy.

Colors are also used quite purposefully. As mentioned before, the color white in "White Tigers" signifies mourning; the narrator in fact refers to the "mourning color." (Kingston, p. 96) Thus, the title implies that tigers are dead because tigers are never white. The color red is used to chase away bad luck. "She tied pretty red yarn around its tail to neutralize the bad luck." (Kingston, p. 96) This detail points to a real Chinese custom and also reinforces the supernatural elements in the novel. In the tale of Fa Mu Lan the narrator paints scenes blue: "When the mountains and the pines turned into blue oxen, blue dogs, and blue people standing, the old couple asked me to spend the night in the hut." (Kingston, p. 26) The color blue provides a supernatural atmosphere. If we look closely at the sentence above, for example, the imagery is surrealistic. The metamorphosis is fanciful as blue is an unusual color for oxen, dogs, and people. Thus the use of the color blue gives the scene a dream-like quality. In "A Story for a Barbarian Reed Pipe," the narrator states, "My silence was thickest - total - during the three years that I covered my school paintings with black paint. I painted layers of black over houses and flowers and suns." (Kingston, p. 192) Black symbolizes her anger, despair, and silence. Thus, color not only makes us visualize the scenes but reinforces the moral fable.

All these devices are evidence of Kingston's artistry. The decisive chapter endings, the suggestive titles, and the symbolic use of colors help to form the structure which reinforces meaning in *The Woman Warrior*. This structure is anything but conventional. Like other modern writers such as John Updike and Joseph Heller, Kingston experiments with form. In Kingston's case her unique form involves an unusual combination of realistic and fantasy elements. Today, in movies such as *Back to the Future, Who Killed Roger Rabbit?*, and *Total Recall*, this superimposed form is fairly commonplace. However, when Kingston was writing in the 1970s this method was far less common. In *The Woman Warrior*, instead of cartoon characters of superheroes, we are given ghosts and legendary figures. Real people are called ghosts, and there are also real ghosts. To understand the use of ghosts in this complex narrative knot, it is necessary to separate all the threads carefully.

The nature of Kingston's artistry is tied to her philosophy of life. In her interview with the *Washington Post*, Kingston explains her narrative style: "I'm an existentialist. The only way I can talk about it is to put it in a dramatic situation." (Allen, p. 4) Kingston's scenes are indeed very dramatic. As Allen points out, "She also puts [scenes] in observations so concrete that fact and meaning become the same: ... how her mother not only couldn't read alphabetic writing, but couldn't see the ducks, cats, and mice in American cartoons; a well in the cellar 'like a wobble of black jello.'" (Allen, p. 4) This vividness is anything but accidental. Kingston has said, "It takes me nine rewrites to get to that immediacy .... The whole analytic process is separate anyway .... Feelings and situations may be very simple. It's analysis which makes them complicated. What I'm writing about is showing the exact way in which the mind works. I want to write according to our brain patterns." (Allen, p. 4) Thus, in Kingston's own words her writing is carefully planned and revised. In addition, she analyzes her writing precisely -nine times before declaring it finished. Each detail contributes to the novel's immediacy. In Paul Gray's formulation, "Though it is drenched in alienation, *The Woman Warrior* never whines. Author Kingston avoids rhetoric for a wealth of detail." (Gray, p. 91) Indeed, the action and imagery are clothed in the most forceful language. The birth scene in "No Name Woman" is but one example among many: "She pulled it up on her belly, and it lay curled there, butt in the air, feet precisely tucked one under the other." (Kingston, p. 17) Here as elsewhere, Kingston's words are like sharpened pebbles as they penetrate the reader's sensibilities.

Thus far by using several microscopes we have reviewed various structural devices in *The Woman Warrior*: contrast between strong and weak characters, decisive chapter endings, revealing chapter titles, different points of view, the significant use of ghosts and the elements of fantasy. How do the above fit together to produce Kingston's moral fable? If we look closely, we can see a meaningful pattern. As mentioned earlier, the strong and the weak are vividly contrasted. As Anju reflects on the models she must choose from, reality and fantasy sometimes overlap and we experience Anju's mixed, even contradictory emotions. For us as for Anju, the climax occurs at the end of the novel when Anju makes her choice to follow the woman warrior's path.

The clue to this moral fable lies in the title *The Woman Warrior*. It is true that the title is derived from one of the characters, Fa Mu Lan. But the title of a book usually does not stand for only one of its characters unless it is a story about that character. In *The Woman Warrior* there are five main characters who are almost equally important. Thus the title primarily stands for the concept of a woman warrior rather than the legendary character in the book. The key to solving this complicated puzzle is to understand the spirit, weapons, and enemies of a woman warrior.

What does the woman warrior's spirit consist of? Her spirit has several characteristics. In the novel Fa Mu Lan leads a virtuous army: "My army did not rape, only taking food where there was an abundance. We brought order wherever we went." (Kingston, p. 44) Thus, the warrior's spirit is not negative but positive. Her first opponent is a giant, which brings to mind the bravery of little David fighting against Goliath. The woman warrior considers herself an avenger rather than an attacker: "I am a female avenger." (Kingston, p. 51) The warrior does not attack but defends what is rightfully hers. Thus, the warrior acts with the spirit of justice. This spirit, the author tells us indirectly, should continue today. The narrator relates Fa Mu Lan's story and then reflects on her own situation. "To avenge my family, I'd have to storm across the United States to take back ... the laundry in New York and the one in California." (Kingston, p. 58) The fact that Anju relates the ancient tale and then compares it to her situation is definitely a strong clue to her theme. The spirit of the legendary warrior should be continued today, but the necessary weapons are different because it is physically impossible for Anju to "storm across the United States."

The weapons that are effective today are not swords but words. The importance of words is stressed several times in the novel. "We are going to carve revenge on your back," her father tells the woman warrior. "We'll write our oaths and names." (Kingston, p. 41) The fact that words are carved on the back of the woman warrior signifies that words are the motivating power behind her skill in battle. The carving is a very long and painful process, but Fa Mu Lan must endure the cutting of the words on her back. "My father first brushed the words in ink, and they fluttered down my back row after row. Then he began cutting; to make fine lines and points he used thin blades, for the stems, large blades."(Kingston, p. 41) The warrior wants to make the connection between words and weapons clear: "When I could sit up again, my mother brought two mirrors, and I saw my back covered entirely with words in red and black files, like an army, like an army." (Kingston, p. 42)

Words are the source of conflict and reconciliation between mother and daughter. The first words of the book are: "'You must not tell anyone,' my mother said, 'what I am about to tell you.'" (Kingston, p. 3) Her mother wants to silence her daughter so much that (in her fantasy) she cuts out her tongue. Later the daughter finally screams, "And I don't want to listen to any more of your stories, they have no logic. They scramble me up.... You can't stop me from talking. You tried to cut off my tongue, but it didn't work." The mother retorts, "'I cut it to make you talk more not less, you dummy!'" (Kingston, p. 235)

However, words are not only a source of conflict but of reconcilation. Using words the mother teaches her daughter Anju the song of the warrior. "Instantly, I remember that as a child I had followed my mother about the house, the two of us singing about how Fa Mu Lan fought gloriously and returned alive from war to settle in the village. I had forgotten this chant that was once mine, given me by my mother, who may not have known its power to remind. She said I would grow up a wife and a slave, but she taught me the song of the warrior woman, Fa Mu Lan. I would have to grow up a warrior woman." (Kingston, p. 24) In this sentence the mother tells Anju to get married and respect her husband, but also to remember the warrior's song because the "song" is the warrior's spirit.

The most important reconcilation occurs at the end of the novel. It is quite significant that in the last paragraph of the book the mother and daughter are telling a story together. "Here is a story my mother told me, not when I was young, but recently, when I told her I also talk story. The beginning is hers, the ending, mine." (Kingston, p. 240) It seems that as the narrator grows older she also comes to "talk story." In other words she becomes more like her mother as she matures. The book starts with the mother talking and ends with the daughter speaking.

The story that they tell together is of particular interest because here we can grasp the moral fable even though it is told indirectly. The story is about Ts'ai, a poetess who lived in 175 A.D. She lived with her captors for twelve years. She could not speak the language and the barbarians laughed at her. Every night she heard the barbarians play flute outside her tent. One night "the barbarians heard a woman's voice singing, as if to her babies, a song so high and clear, it matched the flutes ... Her words seemed to be Chinese but the barbarians understood their sadness and anger. Sometimes they thought they could catch barbarians phrases about forever wandering. Her children did not laugh, but eventually sang along when she left her tent to sit by the winter campfires, ringed by barbarians." (Kingston, p. 243) The situation of the poetess parallels Brave Orchid's. The last lines of the novel are quite significant: "She brought her songs back from the savage lands, and one of the three that has passed down to us is 'Eighteen Stanzas for a Barbarian Reed Pipe,' a song that Chinese sing to their own instruments. It translated well." (Kingston, p. 243) The last words, "It translated well," refer to the book itself. The mother does not speak English but her songs are translated into English by her daughter. Anju, colored by her American perspective, is the narrator and translator of her mother's "talk story." Together the mother and daughter have produced a synthesis of past and present. Using words as her weapons the daughter can carry on the warrior's spirit.

The next requirement of the warrior is that she must carry weapons. A pen rather than a sword is what today's woman warrior should carry. As mentioned before, words are very important in the novel. The old saying "The word is mightier than the sword" seems to be the core of Kingston's message. This message reminds me of Longfellow's words in "A Psalm of Life": "Art is long, and Time is fleeting," and "Act, act in the living present." The reference to Longfellow is not farfetched because the imagery in the last paragraph of *The Woman Warrior* is similar to the last stanza of Longfellow's "The Day is Done": "And the night shall be filled with music/ and the cares, that infest the day/ Shall fold their tents, like the Arabs/ And as silently steal away." The similar imagery leads me to conclude that their messages are also similar. Action is important to Kingston and the activity of writing is an especially vital part of her existence.

The word "warrior" also implies that an enemy exists. Therefore the warrior should carry a shield, for without a shield a warrior will be destroyed. Who or what are the enemies that the five women must encounter in the novel? In "No Name Woman" the villagers attack the pregnant aunt. In "White Tigers" Fa Mu Lan fights against the giant and then the Emperor." In "At the Western Palace" Moon Orchid's husband mocks and rejects her for her old age and ugliness. Classmates taunt Anju for being Chinese. The warrior must also use her shield to defend herself from the many ghosts real or unreal in the novel. All these examples are painful experiences that have wounded Asian Americans for centuries. Thus the warrior should protect herself from allowing these fiery darts to pierce her spirit. Kingston includes portraits of weak characters to show what happens to women who do not do anything to fight back. That is why Anju bursts into anger at the Quiet Girl. That is also why the memory of the No Name Woman affects her like a bothering bee.

The woman warrior's call to action is to use the power of the spoken or written word to overcome her own weaknesses, for it isn't the situation or how others treat her that matters but how she responds. Thus every fear can be a seed of faith and every defeat can be a stepping stone to victory. *The Woman Warrior* is about fighting and how to preserve one's self-esteem and dignity. The Quiet Girl's silence is repulsive to an existentialist (Kingston's self-description), and so Anju beats her mercilessly. Kingston's moral fable is existentialist in the most basic sense. Her call is for the reader to pick up his or her sword of knowledge. This message applies not only to women but to all Americans. As Kingston relates to Islas, "I am really a megalomaniac because I write for everyone living today and people in the future; that's my audience, for generations." (Yalom, p. 16) Although this is Kingston's intention, her message is understood more precisely by Asian Americans as the pain that Anju encounters growing up in Stockton applies to many Asians. Kingston uses women in her first book because she can easily draw upon her own experiences. Her second book, *China Men* (1980), continues the theme of discrimination because this seems to be her primary concern rather than women's rights. (*China Men* is not included in this study because it lacks the vitality of *The Woman Warrior*.)

Thus we have a writer who relies on her own background to create a unique novelistic form. Her style is definitely original and in the American tradition. As an example, Islas points out that Kingston acknowledges William Carlos Williams as a significant influence: "His work 'The American Dream' was the inspiration for her conception of what it means to claim America in a literary way." (Yalom, p. 16) Like Williams, Kingston breaks away from stylistic conventions. Furthermore, Kingston's images are as precise as William's image of a bright red wheelbarrow.

Not only does Kingston claim America in a literary way, she also claims America as rightfully hers. This is an important point to note when one tries to identify her audience. "When

I say I am a native American with all the rights of an American
I am saying, 'No, we're not outsiders; we Chinese belong here.
This is our country, this is our history. We are a part of
America.'" (Yalom, p. 16) Thus her message is aimed at all
Americans. However, because her characters and incidents
are born out of an Asian American heritage, it seems that the
Asian American audience can best identify with her message.
Kingston underlines the difficulties of the Asian American
experience in America and tries to retain what is most
valuable in her heritage. However, her experience is not
simply rejecting one tradition and embracing another.
Indeed, her admiration for the American individualistic
tradition is evident (the hero of her recent novel *Tripmaster
Monkey* [1990] is named Wittman after Walt Whitman).

Kingston's message is conveyed indirectly, but the clues
clearly unfold her fable. *The Woman Warrior* is not simply a
montage of vivid scenes. As we have seen, there is a definite
pattern in characterization and form. This pattern works
toward a reconcilation of form and fable. At the end of the
novel Anju decides to be a strong woman like her mother and
other positive role models. Her mother is a speaker and a
doer. In contrast, Anju is so quiet at the beginning that she
thinks her tongue is tied. She is also reflective. Anju is able to
analyze her own behavior by comparing herself to the other
character models. At the end of the novel Anju finishes a story
tht her mother begins. Thus she is ready to be a contemporary woman warrior. Kingston's own words support this
premise: "They read the beginning and can't understand that
things are resolved by the end. There is a lot of resolution —
the mother and daughter come out okay, you know. But it's at
the price of a lifetime of struggle." (Yalom, p. 14)

Anju enters the battlefield not with a sword but with a pen.
It is clear that the resolution of the moral fable is definitely
linked to the written word: "The daughter becomes the
inheritor of the mother's oral tradition, which subsequently
becomes a written tradition .... 'I went through a time when I
did not talk to people. It's still happening to me but not so
severely. I'm all right now but I do know people who never
came out of it.'" (Yalom, p. 17) Kingston has, indeed, found

her own voice and pen to convey her message. As Thoreau says in *Walden*, "If a man does not keep pace with his companions, perhaps it is because he hears a different drummer. Let him step to the music which he hears, however measured or far away." In this novel Kingston has done just that. She has listened to her own inner spirit and its responses to the world as an Asian American although her work is directed to all Americans. In sum, Kingston's creative form and message define her as one of the most interesting contemporary artists.

Chapter Seven

Conclusion

C.Y. Lee, Kim Yong Ik, Richard Kim, Yoshiko Uchida, and Maxine Hong Kingston have used a wide range of literary tools to accommodate different shapes of belief. In studying their works I have applied the same critical standards usually applied to non-Asian Americans. I have examined under a literary microscope such tools or techniques as point of view, description, dialogue, tone, and figurative language. The forms used by these five Asian American writers to convey their particular beliefs vary from a simple love story in a faraway Korean village to a complicated narrative knot of fantasy and reality. It is evident that these efforts belong to the general family of American literature, but in Asian American literature there are almost always attempts to produce a unique product. As these innovations are seldom explored in any detail, it is not presumptuous to say that this is one of the first literary studies of Asian American literature.

It is a fallacy to put all Asian American authors and audiences into one mold because there are important differences based on factors such as nationality and generation. Thus, each work has been examined on its literary merits. However, it is also a fallacy to assume that there are no features to be distinguished from other American texts. The term "Asian American" suggests distinctive characteristics that are neither simply Asian nor American. For example, the characters in almost all Asian American literature are Asian Americans. These characters reflect Asian American reality and experience. However, depending upon the author's generation, his style and structure vary. For example, the first generation writers were faced with writing in a second language with materials sometimes derived from experiences in their native countries. The second generation writers, however, write from an Asian American perspective.

The question of audience is also relevant. Whom do the Asian American writers address? As Elaine Kim points out, "The challenge that Kingston and other Asian American writers face is how to preserve the artistic integrity of their writing and be understood at the same time by readers whose different cultural experiences might necessitate discourses and explanations that interfere with the art." (Kim, *Asian American Literature*, p. xvii) These writers hope that the whole world will read and understand their works, but I think they also realize the non-Asian American audience may not catch some of the Asian references and allusions. However, though some of these details are not understood fully by non-Asian readers, the value of the work is not seriously compromised. We appreciate their works much as we appeciate the Greek classics though we do not understand all the specific references, or Ezra Pound and T. S. Eliot although we do not catch all the allusions.

These writers may wish to be read by all audiences, but this has proved difficult because historically the American audience has not shown much interest in Asian American literature. As Han points out, "The apathy of American readers toward the literature of Asian immigrants has lasted for almost one and a half centuries." (Han, p. 7) In addition, the number of Asian American readers has been quite small. Most Asian Americans a hundred years ago were more concerned with physical survival than with literature. Today, however, all this is changing. There are departments of Asian American studies developing in several universities and the number of the Asian American audience is increasing rapidly. Furthermore, books about the Asian American experience are in increasing demand. The fact that my five authors have received numerous reviews by well-known critics is quite significant. Maxine Hong Kingston's *The Woman Warrior* was on the best seller lists for a long time, and Amy Tan's *The Joy Luck Club* (1989) and *The Kitchen God's Wife* (1991) are more recent examples of Asian American books high on such lists.

In order to reach the general public these writers use frames and techniques that audiences are familiar with. For the first generation Asian American writers the task was doubly hard. First they had to create a literary work in a second language, then they had to win the approval of a non-Asian American audience. The second generation writers are more American than Asian. As English is their native language, their styles and expressions are clearly communicated to the general public. For both the first generation and second generation writers, there are two overlapping audiences. Both audiences are American, but the Asian American audience can identify more closely with the subject matter.

Nonetheless, it is interesting to note that the most negative criticism has come from critics with the same ethnic background. C. Y. Lee has been accused of perpetuating Chinese stereotypes, and Kingston has been blamed for following a feminist fad. Perhaps this harsh reaction is due to the fact that for a very long time Asian Americans have been portrayed in literature as inferior stereotypes. This same reaction was evident when Black Americans first started writing during the Harlem Renaissance. In 1928 James W. Johnson argued that "the Aframerican author faces a special problem which the plain American author knows nothing about—the problem of the double audience. It is more than a double audience; it is a divided audience, an audience made up of two elements with differences and often opposite and antagonistic points of view." (Scruggs, p. 543) For the Asian American author the double audience consists of members of her own ethnic group and the general American audience. Sometimes, colored by their own judgmental perspectives, the Asian American audience has been quite harsh in their responses while the general audience has often shown apathy toward Asian American literature. It is of great significance, however, that my five writers have penetrated these barriers of hostility and apathy.

Henry James once remarked in a letter to T. S. Perry, "To have not a national stamp has hitherto been a defect and a drawback, but I think it not unlikely that American writers may yet indicate that a vast intellectual fusion and synthesis of the various national tendencies of the world is the condition of

more important achievements than any we have seen."
(Veeder, p. 1) This remark is relevant because the five Asian
American writers discussed here have fused and synthesized
the various aspects of their heritage with their contemporary
experience.   Thus, although these writers have drawn upon
their Asian heritage for their materials, their shapes of belief
are born from a marriage of their Asian heritage and their
American experience. Emerson says of the American Scholar,
"He is the world's eye. He is the world's heart." To the extent
the writers in this study have realized Emerson's ideal, they
have a just claim to be seen as the pioneers of Asian American
literature.

Bibliography of Works Cited

Allen, Henry, "Warrior's Luck." *Washington Post*. 26 June 1980. Sec. D 4

Aristotle, *The Complete Works of Aristotle*. Vol. Two, Ed. Jonathan Barnes. Princeton, New Jersey: Princeton University Press, 1984.

Baker, Houston A. Jr., ed. *Three American Literatures: Essays on Chicano, Native Americans and Asian American Literature for Teachers of American Literature*. New York: MLA, 1982.

Booth, Wayne C. *The Rhetoric of Fiction*. Chicago: University of Chicago Press. Rev. Ed. 1983.

Burnett, Hallie and Whit. *Fiction Writer's Handbook*. New York: Harper & Row, 1975.

Camus, Albert. *The Plague* New York: Alfred A. Knopf, 1969.

Chin, Jeffrey Paul and others. "Resources for Chinese and Japanese American Literary Traditions" *Amerasia*. 1 (1981) 19-31.

Chin, Frank, Jeffrey Pual Chan, Lawson Fusao Inada, Shawn Hsu Wong, *Aiiieeeee*. Washington, D. C.: Howard University Press, 1974.

Colby, Jean Poindexter. *Writing, Illustrating & Editing Children's Books*. New York: Hasting House, 1976.

Crane, Ronald. "The Concept of Plot" *The Theory of the Novel.* Ed. Philip Stevick New York: The Free Press, 1967. 141-145

Daniels, Roger. *Asian America.* Seattle: University of Washington Press, 1988.

Dasenbrock, Reed Way. "Intelligibility and Meaningfulness in Multicultural Literature in English" *PMLA.* (Jan. 1987) Vol 1. No. 102 1-15.

Dickinson, Emily. "After great pain, a formal feeling comes." *The New Oxford Book of American Verse.* Ed. Richard Ellmann, New York: Oxford University Press, 1976.

_____ "I felt a Funeral, in my Brain." *The New Oxford Book of American Verse.* Ed. Richard Ellmann, New York: Oxford University Press, 1976.

Finkelstein, Sidney. *Existentialism and Alienation in Literature.* New York; International Publishers, 1965.

Fisher, Dexter ed. *The Third Women.* New York: Houghton Mifflin Co., 1980.

Friedman, Norman. *Form and Meaning in Fiction.* Athens: University of Georgia Press, 1975.

_____ "Point of View in Fiction" *The Theory of the Novel.* New York: The Free Press, 1967. 108-137.

Gallagher, Kent. C. *The Foreigner in Early American Drama.* Hague: Mouton & Co., 1966.

Gong, Ted. "Approaching Cultural Change through Literature From Chinese to Chinese American." *Amerasia* (1980) 73-80.

Gordon, Mary. "Mythic History" *New York Times Book Review.* 15 June 1980. 23.

Gray, Paul. "Book Review." *Time*. 16 December 1976.

Gross, Theodore, ed. *A Nation of Nations*. New York: The Free Press, 1971.

Han, Hsaio-min. "Roots and Buds: The Literature of Chinese Americans" unpublished diss. Brigham Young University, 1980.

Haslam, Gerald W. *Forgotten Pages of American Literature*. Boston: Houghton Mifflin Co., 1970.

Hoefer, Hans Johannes. *Korea*. Hong Kong: Apa Productions, 1981.

Holman, C. Hugh, and William Harmon. *A Handbook to Literature*. New York: Macmillan Publishing, Co., 1986.

Holte, James Craig, *The Ethnic I*. Westport, Conn: Greenwood Press, 1988.

Hom, Marlon K. "A Case of Mutual Exclusion. Portrayals by Immigrants and American Born Chinese of Each Other in Literature." *Amerasia*. 11 (1984): 29-45.

Hsaio, Ruth B. "The Stages of Development in American Ethnic Literature: Jewish and Chinese American Literatures" Dissertation, Tufts University, May 1986.

Hsu, Kai-yi and Helen Palubinsakas, eds. *Asian American Authors*. Boston: Houghton, 1976.

Ichioka, Yuji. *The Issei*. New York: Free Press 1988.

Irwin, Hadley & Jeannette Eyerly. *Writing Young Adult's Novels*. Cinn: Writers Digest Books, 1988.

Islas, Arturo. "An Interview Between Kingston and Arturo Islas." *Women Writers of the West Coast*. Marilyn Yalom Ed. Santa Barbara: Capra Press, 1983.

James, Thomas. *Exile Within*. Cambridge, Mass: Harvard University Press, 1987.

Juhasz, Suzanne. "Maxine Hong Kingston Narrative Technique in Female Identity." *Contemporary American Women Writers* Catherine Rainwater and William J. Schenck, eds.University of Kentucky Press, 1985. 173-189.

Kim, Elaine. *Asian American Literature*. Philadelphia: Temple University Press., 1982.

_____ "Visions and Fierce Dreams: A Commentary on the Works of Maxine Hong Kingston." *Amerasia* (1982): 145-162.

Kim, Richard E. *Lost Names*. New York: Praeger Publishing 1970.

_____ "Introduction" *The Martyred*. Seoul: Sisayongosa Inc. Press (no date)

_____ *The Martyred*. New York: Pocket Books, 1965.

Kim, Yong Ik "A Book-Writing Venture" From Our Rostrum *Writer* October, 1965.

_____ "Love in Winter" *Love in Winter*. Seoul: Korea University Press, 1963.

_____ "The Wedding Shoes" *Love in Winter*. Seoul: Korea University Press, 1963.

_____ "From Here You Can See the Moon" Seoul: Korea University Press, 1963.

Kingston, Maxine Hong. *China Men* New York: Ballantine Books, 1981.

_____ *Tripmaster Monkey*. New York: Vintage Press, 1990.

_____ *The Woman Warrior*. New York: Vintage Press, 1976.

Klinkowitz, Jerome. *The New American Novel of Manners*. Athens: University of Georgia Press, 1986.

Kraemer, Casper J. Jr. *The Complete Works of Horace*. New York: Random House 1936.

Kwong, Peter. *The New Chinatown*. New York: Noonday Press, 1989.

Lee, Chin Yang Lee. *Flower Drum Song*. New York: Farrar, Straus, Cudahy, Inc. 1957.

_____ *Lover's Point*. New York: Farrar, Straus, Cudahy, Inc. 1958.

Lee, Mary Paik. *Quiet Odyssey*. Seattle: University of Washington Press, 1990.

Lim, Shirley Geok-lin and others, ed. *The Forbidden Stitch: An American Women's Anthology*. Corvallis, Oregon: Calyx Books, 1989.

Lin, Yutang. *My Country and My People*. New York: John Day Co., 1937.

Lowe, C. H. *Facing Adversitites with a Smile*. San Francisco, Chinese Materials Center Publication, 1984.

Lubbock, Percy. *The Craft of Fiction*. New York: Cape & Harrison Smith, 1981.

Lyman, Stanford M. *Chinese Americans*. New York: Random House, 1974.

McCurdy, John Chang. *Koran Fantasia.* Seoul: Seoul International Publishing House, (no. date).

Mizener, Arthur. *The Sense of Life.* New York: Houghton Mifflin Co., 1964.

Nakao, Annie "Nisei Author's Gift to Children." *San Francisco Examiner.* 29, Sept. 1989.

Oakes, Whitney J. and Eugene O'Neill, Jr. *The Complete Greek Drama.* Vol. One. New York: Random House, 1938.

Pai, Margaret K. *The Dreams of Two Yi Min.* Honolulu: University of Hawaii Press, 1989.

Pearson, Carol and Katherine Pope. *The Female Hero in American and British Literature.* New York: R.R. Bowker Co., 1961.

Pfaff, Timothy. "Talk with Mrs. Kingston" *New York Times Book Review.* 15 June 1980. 9.

Robertson, Nan. "Ghosts of Girlhood Lift Obscure Book to Peak of Acclaim." *New York Times.* 12 Feb. 1977, 26.

Rockwell, F. A. *Modern Fiction Techniques.* Boston: The Writer Inc. 1962.

Rosenfield, Isaac. "In the Role of the Writer and the Little Magazine" *The Chicago Review Anthology.* Ed. David Ray. University of Chicago Press. 1959.

Sacks, Sheldon. *Fiction and the Shape of Belief.* Berkeley: University of California Press, 1964.

Sartre, Jean Paul. *What is Literature?* London: Methuen and Co., 1948.

Schopen, Bernard A. "The Aesthetics of Ambiguity: The Novels of John Updike." UNR Diss. 1975.

Scruggs, Charles. "All Dressed Up But No Place To Go" *American Literature*. 48 (Jan. 1977) 543.

Shirota, Jon. *Pineapple White*. Los Angeles: Ohara Publications, 1972.

Sledge, Linda Ching. "Teaching Asian American Literature" *ADE Bulletin*. (Spring 1985): 42-45.

Sloane, William. *The Craft of Writing*. New York: W.W. Norton & Co., 1979.

Sollors, Werner. *Beyond Ethnicity*. Oxford: Oxford University Press, 1986.

Sowell, Thomas. *Ethnic America*. New York: Bask Books, 1981.

Stevick, Philip. *The Theory of the Novel*. New York: The Fress, 1967.

Sumida, Stephen H. "Reviews" *Amerasia* 11 (1984):105-109.

Surmelian, Leon. *Techniques of Fiction Writing*. New York: Doubleday & Co., 1968.

Takaki, Ronald. *Iron Cages*. New York: Oxford University Press, 1990.

_____ *Strangers from a Different Shore*. Boston: Little Brown & Co., 1989

Tan, Amy. *The Joy Luck Club*. New York: Putnan & Sons, 1989.

Thody, Philip *Albert Camus*. New York: St. Martin's Press. 1989.

_____ *Albert Camus 1913-60*. London: Hamilton, 1961.

Tuttleton, James W. *The Novels of Manners in America*. North Carolina: University of North Carolina Press, 1972.

Uchida, Yoshiko. *A Jar of Dreams*. New York: Scribner Publishing, 1971.

_____ *Journey Home*. New York: Atheneum Press, 1978.

_____ *Journey to Topaz*. New York: Scribner Publishing, 1971.

_____ *Picture Bride*. New York: Simon and Schuster, 1987.

Veeder, William, ed. *The Art of Criticism*. Chicago, University of Chicago Press, 1980.

Vivante, Arturo *Writing Fiction*. Boston: The Writer Inc. 1980.

Wang, David Hsin-Fu ed., *Asian American Heritage*. New York: Washington Square Press, 1974.

Whitney, Phyllis A. *Writing Juvenile Stories and Novels*. Boston: The Writer Inc. 1976.

Wilbers, Stephen. *The Iowa's Writers' Workshop*. Iowa: University of Iowa Press, 1980.

Wong, Nellie. "Woman Warrior: Memoirs of a Girlhood Among Ghosts" *Bridge*. (Winter 1978): 46-48.

Wu, William F. *The Yellow Peril*. New York: Archon Books 1982.

Yalom, Marilyn ed. *Women Writers of the West Coast*. Santa Barbara: Capra Press, 1983.

Yee, Paul. *Tales from Gold Mountain*. New York: Macmillan 1989.

Yeh, Michelle. "Metaphor and Bi Western and Chinese Poetics." *Comparative Literature*. 39 (Summer 1987): 239-252.

Yu, Jong-ho "Introduction." *The Cruel City*. Seoul: Sisayon-gosa Publishers, 1983.

Zong, Insob. *A Guide to Korean Literature*. New Jersey: Hollym, 1988.